U.S. Department of Justice
Office of Justice Programs
Bureau of Justice Statistics

Revised 6/30/2010

Bureau of Justice Statistics

BULLETIN

December 2009, NCJ 228417

Prisoners in 2008

William J. Sabol, Ph.D., and
Heather C. West, Ph.D., *BJS Statisticians*
Matthew Cooper, *BJS Intern*

At yearend 2008, federal and state correctional authorities had jurisdiction over 1,610,446 prisoners (figure 1). *Jurisdiction* refers to the legal authority over a prisoner, regardless of where the prisoner is held.

The prison population increased by 12,201 prisoners from 2007 to 2008, the smallest annual increase since 2000. The 0.8% growth during 2008 was the second year of decline in the rate of growth and the slowest growth in eight years. From 2000 to 2008 the growth of the prison population (1.8% per year on average) was less than a third of the rate observed during the 1990s (6.5% per year on average) (not shown in figure).

State correctional authorities had jurisdiction over 1,409,166 prisoners at yearend 2008, an increase of 10,539 state prisoners during the year. Federal correctional authorities (or the federal prison system) had jurisdiction over 201,280 prisoners, up 1,662 federal prisoners from the previous year. While the numbers of state and federal prisoners reached all-time yearend highs in 2008, the respective growth rates for each slowed to 0.8% (figure 2). This was the second

smallest annual rate of growth in the state prison population (0.1% growth occurred in 2001) and the lowest rate for the federal prison population since 2000.

> Detailed information is included in the appendix tables, following *Methodology.* Topics covered in the appendix tables are shown on page 14.

Figure 1.

Prisoners under state or federal jurisdiction at yearend, 2000-2008

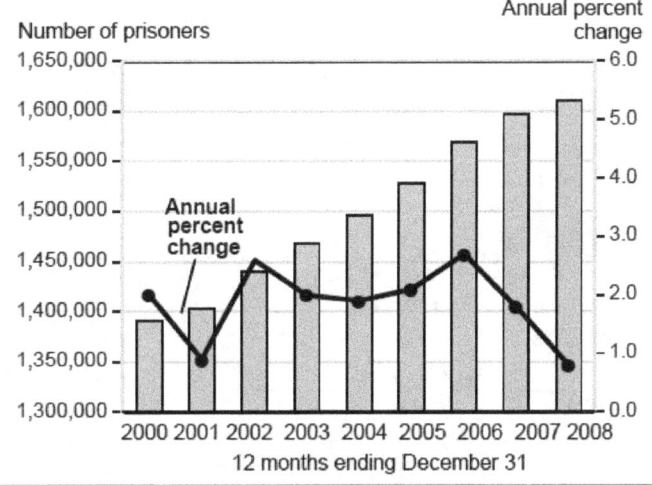

Highlights

- The U.S. prison population grew at the slowest rate (0.8%) since 2000, reaching 1,610,446 prisoners at yearend 2008.

- Growth of the prison population since 2000 (1.8% per year on average) was less than a third of the average annual rate during the 1990s (6.5% per year on average).

- Slower growth in the state prison population was associated with fewer new court commitments during 2007 and 2008, reversing the trend of steady growth of state prison admissions witnessed from 2000 to 2006.

- An increase in the number of prison releases was led by offenders released to the community without supervision.

- Between 2000 and 2008 the number of blacks in prison declined by 18,400, lowering the imprisonment rate to 3,161 men and 149 women per 100,000 persons in the U.S. resident black population.

- The U.S. imprisonment rate declined for the second time since yearend 2000; about 1 in every 198 persons in the U.S. resident population was incarcerated in state or federal prison at yearend 2008.

Twenty states reported a decline in the number of prisoners under their jurisdiction in 2008 for a total decrease of 9,719 prisoners (appendix table 2). New York (down 2,273 prisoners), Georgia (down 1,537), and Michigan (down 1,495) reported the largest reductions, accounting for more than half (54.6%) of the decline in the total number of prisoners. New York (down 3.6%) recorded the largest rate of decrease in its prison population during 2008, followed by Kentucky (down 3.3%), and New Jersey (down 3.3%).

Twenty-nine states and the federal prison system reported a combined increase of 21,920 prisoners at yearend. Pennsylvania (up 4,178 prisoners) and Florida (up 4,169) had the largest increases, followed by Arizona (1,843), the federal prison system (1,662), and North Carolina (1,512). Combined, these five jurisdictions accounted for 61% of the growth among jurisdictions holding more prisoners at yearend. Pennsylvania also reported the fastest rate of growth (up 9.1%) for 2008.

Figure 2.

Percent change in number of prisoners under state or federal jurisdiction, 2000-2008

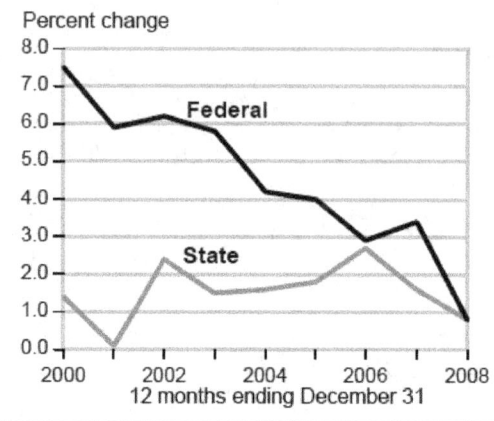

Selected characteristics of the prison population under state and federal jurisdiction

• Men were 93% of prisoners under state or federal jurisdiction, and women were 7% (table 1).

• About 34% of all sentenced prisoners were white, 38% were black, and 20% were Hispanic.

• Males were imprisoned at a rate about 15 times higher than females (table 2).

• Black males were imprisoned at a rate six and half times higher than white males.

Table 1.

Number of prisoners under state and federal jurisdiction, by sentence length, race, Hispanic origin, and gender, 2008

	Total	Male	Female
Prisoners by sentence length			
Total under jurisdiction	1,610,446	1,495,594	114,852
Sentenced to more than 1 year	1,540,036	1,434,784	105,252
Estimated prisoners by race[a]			
White[b]	528,200	477,500	50,700
Black[b]	591,900	562,800	29,100
Hispanic	313,100	295,800	17,300

[a]Based on prisoners sentenced to more than 1 year. Excludes American Indians, Alaska Natives, Asians, Native Hawaiians, other Pacific Islanders, and persons identifying two or more races.

[b]Excludes persons of Hispanic or Latino origin.

Table 2.

Imprisonment rate per 100,000 person in the U.S. resident population, by race, Hispanic origin, and gender, 2008

	Male	Female
Total[a]	952	68
White[b]	487	50
Black[b]	3,161	149
Hispanic	1,200	75

Note: Imprisonment rates are the number of prisoners under state or federal jurisdiction sentenced to more than 1 year per 100,000 persons in the U.S. resident population in the referenced population group. See *Methodology* for estimation method.

[a]Total includes American Indians, Alaska Natives, Asians, Native Hawaiians, other Pacific Islanders, and persons identifying two or more races.

[b]Excludes persons of Hispanic or Latino origin.

Slower growth in the state prison population associated with fewer new court commitments

Several factors contributed to slowing the growth of the state and federal prison populations from 2006 to 2008, including a decrease in the number of prison admissions, a decline in the number of new court commitments to state prison, and an increase in the number released from both state and federal prison. Prison admissions have declined for the past two years as the number of admissions dropped by about 6,923 sentenced offenders during 2007 and by 3,743 prisoners during 2008 (table 3).

The number of offenders released from state and federal prisons rose by 2.0% to reach 735,454 prisoners while the number of admissions declined by 0.5% (down 3,743).

Among the states, admissions and releases of sentenced prisoners have converged since 2006 as admissions declined and releases of state prisoners increased (figure 3). In 2008, 30 states reported a decrease in prisons admissions, totaling 19,019 prisoners. The remaining 20 states reported an increase in prison admissions, totalling 15,783 prisoners. Four states accounted for 40.7% of the total decrease in prison admissions from 2007 to 2008 (appendix table 11). Georgia (down 2,509) reported the largest absolute decrease, followed by Mississippi (down 1,841), Kansas (down 1,408), and Washington (down 1,229).

Fewer new court commitments to state prison accounted for the declining number of state prison admissions in 2007 and 2008, reversing the trend in the increasing number of state prison admissions observed from 2000 to 2006 (figure 4).[1] The number of new court commitments to state prison dropped by 10,587 in 2007 and 2,189 in 2008 as the total number of state prison admissions declined by 3,046 and 3,787, respectively. The number of parole violators admitted to state prison increased during 2008 at a slower rate than during the previous two years, offsetting some of the effect of the decline in new court commitments on the total number of state prison admissions.

[1]New court commitments include felony offenders sentenced to state prison and probation violators entering prison for the first time on a violation of a condition of probation. Parole violators include any conditionally released parolee admitted to prison either for a technical violation of the conditions of supervision or for a new crime.

Table 3.

Number of sentenced prisoners admitted to and released from state and federal jurisdiction, 2000-2008

Year	Admissions			Releases		
	Total	Federal	State	Total	Federal	State
2000	625,219	43,732	581,487	604,858	35,259	569,599
2001	638,978	45,140	593,838	628,626	38,370	590,256
2002	661,712	48,144	613,568	630,176	42,339	587,837
2003	686,437	52,288	634,149	656,384	44,199	612,185
2004	699,812	52,982	646,830	672,202	46,624	625,578
2005	733,009	56,057	676,952	701,632	48,323	653,309
2006	749,798	57,495	692,303	713,473	47,920	665,553
2007	742,875	53,618	689,257	721,161	48,764	672,397
2008	739,132	53,662	685,470	735,454	52,348	683,106
Average annual change, 2000-2007	2.5%	3.0%	2.5%	2.5%	4.7%	2.4%
Percent change, 2007-2008	-0.5	0.1	-0.5	2.0	7.3	1.6

Note: Totals based on prisoners with a sentence of more than 1 year. Totals exclude transfers, escapes, and AWOLS.

Figure 3.

Number of state admissions and releases and change in number of sentenced state prisoners, December 2000-2008

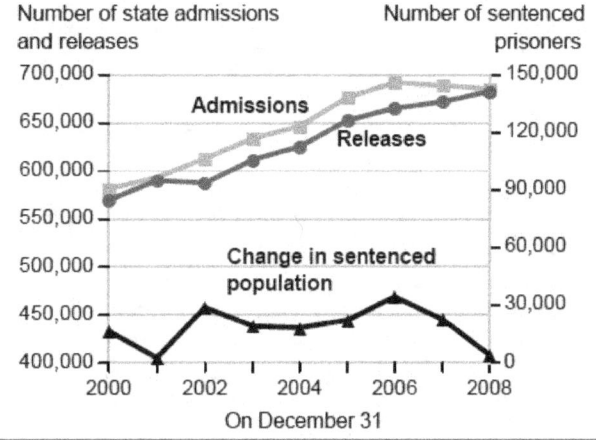

Figure 4.

Sentenced admissions into state prisons, by type of admission, 2000-2008

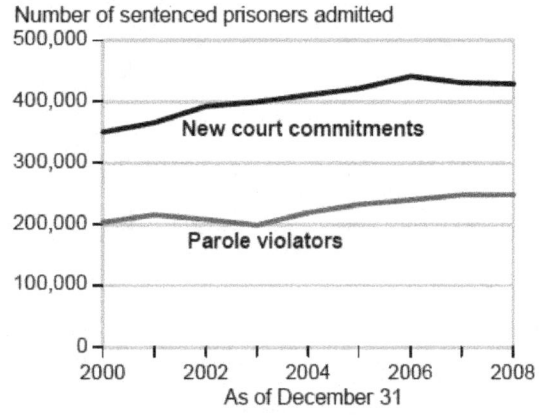

Number and rate of prison releases increased in 2008

The number of offenders released from state and federal prisons increased by 2% (or 14,293 releases) during 2008 to reach 735,454. In total, 29 states and the federal system reported increases in the number of prison releases totaling 23,524 offenders. This increase was offset by a total decrease of 9,034 releases in the remaining 21 states (appendix table 11). The increase in the number of prison releases was led by an 8% (or 16,883 releases) increase in the number of prisoners released unconditionally during 2008.[2]

[2]Unconditional releases include expirations of sentence, commutations, and other unconditional releases.

Table 4.

Number of sentenced prisoners released from state prisons, by type of release, 2000-2008

Year	Releases		
	Total[a]	Conditional[b]	Unconditional[c]
2000	569,599	425,887	118,886
2001	590,256	437,251	130,823
2002	587,837	440,842	127,389
2003	612,185	442,168	127,386
2004	625,578	480,727	123,147
2005	653,309	495,370	133,943
2006	665,553	497,801	148,114
2007	672,397	504,181	152,589
2008	683,106	505,168	165,568

[a]Totals based on prisoners with a sentence of more than 1 year. Totals exclude transfers, escapes, and AWOLS.

[b]Total conditional releases include releases to probation, parole, supervised mandatory releases, and other unspecified conditional releases.

[c]Total unconditional releases include expirations of sentence, commutations, and other unconditional releases.

Unconditional releases from state prisons accounted for 91% of the increase in the total number of prisoners released unconditionally (not shown in a table). During 2008 the number released unconditionally from state prisons increased by about 13,000 (or 8.5%), while conditional releases from state prisons increased by fewer than 1,000 (or about 0.2%) (table 4).[3] As a result of the increase in unconditional releases from state prisons, the share of all state prison admissions accounted for by unconditional releases reached 24% in 2008, a higher share than any year since 2000.

Slower growth in the prison population since 2000 was associated with a decline in the number of sentenced black prisoners

A decrease in the number of sentenced black offenders has been associated with slower growth in the size of the state and federal prison populations. The number of imprisoned blacks has declined by about 18,400 since yearend 2000, reducing the total number of blacks in prison to about 591,900 at yearend 2008 (table 5). Conversely, the numbers of sentenced white and Hispanic offenders have increased since 2000. the number of imprisoned whites has risen by 57,200 since 2000 to reach 528,200 at yearend 2008. The total number of imprisoned Hispanics rose by 96,200 to reach 313,100 during this period.

[3]Conditional releases include releases to probation, supervised mandatory release, and other unspecified conditional releases.

A decrease in the black imprisonment rates accompanied the decline in the number of imprisoned black offenders (table 6). Between 2000 and 2008 the imprisonment rate for black men decreased from 3,457 per 100,000 in the U.S. resident population to 3,161, and the imprisonment rate for black women declined from 205 per 100,000 in the U.S. resident population to 149. For Hispanic men the imprisonment rate remained relatively steady at about 1,200 per 100,000 in the U.S. resident population during this period. For white men the imprisonment rate increased from 449 per 100,000 in the U.S. resident population in 2000 to 487 per 100,000 in 2008.

The decline in the black imprisonment rate since 2000 means that an estimated 61,000 fewer blacks were in state or federal prisons than expected at yearend 2008 if the imprisonment rate for blacks had remained at its 2000 level (not shown in table). In contrast, the increase in the imprisonment rate for whites resulted in about 54,000 more sentenced white prisoners at yearend 2008 than expected if their rate of imprisonment had remained unchanged since 2000. The number of imprisoned Hispanics and the Hispanic U.S. resident population experienced about the same rates of growth from 2000 to 2008. Consequently, there was relatively little difference (3,600) between the number of sentenced Hispanics who would have been in prison in 2008 if the Hispanic imprisonment rate had remained at its 2000 level.

Table 5.

Estimated number of sentenced prisoners under state or federal jurisdiction, by race and Hispanic origin, December 31, 2000-2008

Year	Total number of prisoners			
	Total[a]	White[b]	Black[b]	Hispanic
2000	1,321,200	471,000	610,300	216,900
2001	1,344,500	485,400	622,200	209,900
2002	1,380,300	472,200	622,700	250,000
2003	1,409,300	493,400	621,300	268,100
2004	1,433,800	491,800	583,400	275,600
2005	1,461,100	505,500	577,100	294,900
2006	1,502,200	527,100	562,800	308,000
2007	1,532,800	521,900	586,200	318,800
2008	1,540,100	528,200	591,900	313,100

Note: Totals based on prisoners with a sentence of more than 1 year. See *Methodology* for estimation method.

[a]Includes American Indians, Alaska Natives, Asians, Native Hawaiians, other Pacific Islanders, and persons identifying two or more races.

[b]Excludes persons of Hispanic or Latino origin.

Table 6.

Estimated rate of sentenced prisoners under state or federal jurisdiction, per 100,000 U.S. residents, by gender, race, and Hispanic origin, December 31, 2000-2008

Year	Males				Females			
	Total[a]	White[b]	Black[b]	Hispanic	Total[a]	White[b]	Black[b]	Hispanic
2000	904	449	3,457	1,220	59	34	205	60
2001	896	462	3,535	1,177	58	36	199	61
2002	912	450	3,437	1,176	61	35	191	80
2003	915	465	3,405	1,231	62	38	185	84
2004	926	463	3,218	1,220	64	42	170	75
2005	929	471	3,145	1,244	65	45	156	76
2006	943	487	3,042	1,261	68	48	148	81
2007	955	481	3,138	1,259	69	50	150	79
2008	952	487	3,161	1,200	68	50	149	75

Note: Totals based on prisoners sentenced to more than 1 year. Imprisonment rates are per 100,000 U.S. residents in each reference population group. See *Methodology* for estimation method.

[a]Includes American Indians, Alaska Natives, Asians, Native Hawaiians, other Pacific Islanders, and persons identifying two or more races.

[b]Excludes persons of Hispanic or Latino origin.

Fewer blacks imprisoned for drug offenses accounted for most of the decline in the number of sentenced blacks in state prison

From 2000 to 2006 (the most recent offense data available), the total number of sentenced offenders in state prisons increased by 124,700 to reach 1,331,100 state prisoners. Offenders convicted of a violent offense accounted for 63% of the growth in the state prison population; offenders convicted of a drug offense accounted for about 12% (table 7). The number of sentenced blacks in state prisons fell to 508,700 in 2006, declining by 53,300 prisoners since 2000. More than half of this decline (56%) was made up of 29,600 fewer blacks imprisoned for drug offenses.

Table 7.

Change in number of sentenced prisoners in state prisons, 2000 to 2006, by race and Hispanic origin and offense

Race and Hispanic origin	Number of prisoners in 2006	Change since 2000	Percent of total change
Total offenses	1,331,100	124,700	100.0%
Violent	667,900	78,800	63.2
Property	277,900	39,400	31.6
Drugs	265,800	14,700	11.8
Other[b]	119,500	-8,200	-6.6
White[a]	474,200	37,500	100%
Violent	227,500	15,100	40.3
Property	126,200	17,600	46.9
Drugs	72,000	13,800	36.8
Other[b]	48,500	-9,000	-24.0
Black[a]	508,700	-53,300	100%
Violent	267,900	-5,500	10.3
Property	89,700	-7,100	13.3
Drugs	115,700	-29,600	55.5
Other[b]	35,400	-11,100	20.8
Hispanic or Latino	248,900	70,400	100%
Violent	141,600	54,500	77.4
Property	32,800	4,400	6.3
Drugs	54,100	10,800	15.3
Other[b]	20,400	700	1.0

Note: Data are for inmates sentenced to more than 1 year under the jurisdiction of state correctional authorities. The estimates for gender were based on jurisdiction counts at yearend (NPS 1B). The estimates by race and Hispanic origin were based on data from the 2004 Survey of Inmates in State Correctional Facilities and updated by yearend jurisdiction counts; estimates within offense categories were based on offense distributions from the National Corrections Reporting Program, 2006, updated by yearend jurisdiction counts. All estimates were rounded to the nearest 100. Detail may not add to total due to rounding.

[a]Excludes persons of Hispanic or Latino origin.

[b]Includes public order and other unspecified offenses.

The number of sentenced white and Hispanic prisoners convicted of a drug offense increased from 2000 to 2006, offsetting the decline in the number of imprisoned black drug offenders. Imprisoned white drug offenders increased by 13,800 prisoners during this period; the number of Hispanic drug offenders increased by 10,800. Consequently, the overall number of sentenced drug offenders in state prison increased by 14,700 prisoners.

Changes in the types of drugs involved in drug offenses could not be identified in the available data. BJS's most recent survey focusing on the types of drugs involved in drug offenses was conducted in 2004. The data collected through inmate interviews revealed an increase in the percentage of state prisoners serving time for drug law violations involving stimulants, such as methamphetamines. About 10% of the drug offenders in state prison in 2004 were convicted of a drug offense involving stimulants, up from 10% in 1997. Additionally, the percentage of state prisoners convicted of a cocaine-related drug offense declined from 72% in 1997 to 62% in 2004.[4]

The U.S. imprisonment rate decreased for the second time since yearend 2000

The imprisonment rate at yearend 2008 was 504 per 100,000 U.S. residents, a decrease from 506 per 100,000 at yearend 2007 (appendix table 10). About 1 in every 198 persons in the U.S. resident population was incarcerated in state or federal prison at yearend 2008. *Imprisonment rate* refers to the number of prisoners sentenced to more than 1 year per 100,000 U.S. residents.

A decrease in the imprisonment rate resulted from a lower rate of growth in the sentenced prison population (0.5% increase) than in the U.S. resident population (0.8% increase). This was the second decline in the U.S. imprisonment rate since 2000.

---

[4]See *Drug Use and Dependence, State and Federal Prisoners, 2004* , BJS Web. 11 Oct. 2006.

Twenty-eight states reported a decrease in their imprisonment rates, 20 states reported an increase, and two states reported no change to their imprisonment rates at yearend 2008 (figure 5). Massachusetts and Texas (both down 31 prisoners per 100,000 U.S. residents) reported the largest declines in their imprisonment rates.

Pennsylvania (up 28 prisoners per 100,000), Florida (up 21 prisoners per 100,000), and Alabama (up 19 prisoners per 100,000) reported the largest increases in their imprisonment rates at yearend.

Figure 5.

Change in imprisonment rate, 2007-2008

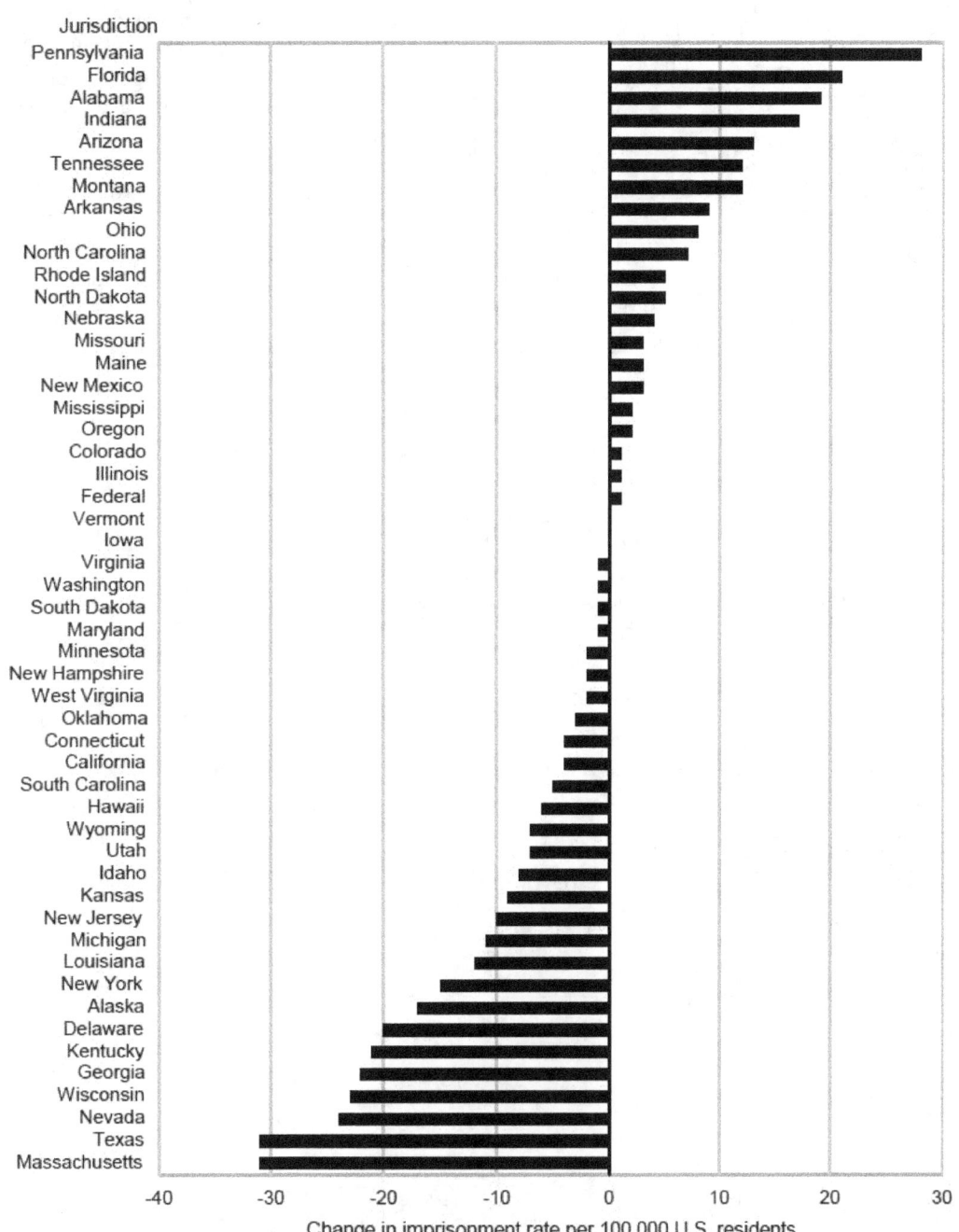

Note: The 2008 imprisonment rate included 4,012 male prisoners sentenced to more than 1 year but held in local jails or houses of corrections in the Commonwealth of Massachusetts; the 2007 imprisonment rate included 6,200 sentenced males held in local jails or houses of corrections. See Methodology.

Selected characteristics of the custody population at yearend 2008

On December 31, 2008—

- State and federal prisons and local jails had custody or physical guardianship over 2,304,115 inmates, an increase of 0.3% from yearend 2007 (table 8).

- About 1 in every 133 U.S. residents was in custody of state or federal prisons or local jails.

- The incarceration rate—the number of inmates held in custody of state or federal prisons or in local jails per 100,000 U.S. residents—decreased to 754 inmates at year-end 2008, down from 756 inmates at yearend 2007.

- The total incarcerated population reached 2,424,279 inmates—up 0.2% or 5,038 inmates from yearend 2007 (table 9).

- Populations held in ICE facilities (up 2.4%) and in local jails (up 0.7%) increased during 2008. The largest absolute increase of inmates occurred in local jails (5,382), followed by state and federal prisons (692).

- Populations held in military facilities (down 8.0%), prisons in U.S. territories (down 7.5%), and jails in Indian country (down 1.3%) decreased. The largest absolute decrease of 1,102 inmates occurred in the U.S. territories during 2008.

Table 8.

Inmates held in custody in state or federal prisons or in local jails, December 31, 2000, 2007, and 2008

Inmates in custody	Number of inmates			Percent of inmates	
	12/31/2000	12/31/2007	12/31/2008	Average annual change, 2000-2007	Percent change, 2007-2008
Total[a]	1,937,482	2,298,041	2,304,115	2.5 %	0.3 %
Federal prisoners[b]					
Total	140,064	197,285	198,414	5.0 %	0.6 %
Prisons	133,921	189,154	189,770	5.1	0.3
Federal facilities	124,540	165,975	165,252	4.2	-0.4
Privately operated facilities	9,381	23,179	24,518	13.8	5.8
Community Corrections Centers[c]	6,143	8,131	8,644	4.1	6.3
State prisoners[a]	1,176,269	1,320,582	1,320,145	1.7 %	0.0 %
Local jails[d]	621,149	780,174	785,556	3.3 %	0.7 %
Incarceration rate[a,e]	684	756	754	1.4 %	-0.3 %

[a]Total includes all inmates held in state or federal prison facilities or in local jails. It does not include inmates held in U.S. territories, military facilities, U.S. Immigration and Customs Enforcement (ICE) facilities, jails in Indian country, and juvenile facil ties.

[b]After 2001 the responsibility for sentenced felons from the District of Columbia was transferred to the Federal Bureau of Prisons.

[c]Non-secure, privately operated community corrections centers.

[d]Counts for inmates held in local jails are for the last weekday of June in each year. Counts were estimated from the Annual Survey of Jails. See *Methodology*.

[e]The total number in custody of state or federal prison facilities or local jails per 100,000 U.S. residents. Resident population estimates were as of January 1 of the following year for December 31 estimates.

Table 9.

Total incarcerated population, December 31, 2007 and 2008

Incarcerated population	Number of inmates		Percent change, 2007-2008
	2007	2008	
Total[a]	2,419,241	2,424,279	0.2%
Federal and state prisons	1,517,867	1,518,559	0.0
Territorial prisons	14,678	13,576	-7.5
Local jails[b]	780,174	785,556	0.7
ICE facilities	9,720	9,957	2.4
Military facilities	1,794	1,651	-8.0
Jails in Indian country	2,163	2,135	-1.3
Juvenile facilities[c]	92,845	92,845	:

:Not calculated.

[a]Total includes all inmates held in state or federal public prison facilities, local jails, U.S. territories, military facilities, U.S. Immigration and Customs Enforcement (ICE) owned and contracted facilities, jails in Indian country, and juvenile facilities.

[b]Counts for inmates held in local jails are for the last weekday of June in each year.

[c]Data are from the 2006 Census of Juveniles in Residential Placement (CJRP), conducted by the Office of Juvenile Justice Delinquency Prevention, Office of Justice Programs, U.S. Department of Justice.

Men ages 30 to 34 and women ages 35 to 39 had the highest imprisonment rates

At yearend 2008, 1,434,800 men and 105,300 women were serving prison sentences of more than one year (appendix table 13). Men ages 25 to 29 represented the largest share (17.2%) of sentenced male prisoners in state or federal prison. The imprisonment rate for men was highest for those ages 30 to 34 (2,366 per 100,000 men in the U.S. resident population), followed by men ages 25 to 29 (2,238 per 100,000) (appendix table 14).

Women ages 35 to 39 made up the largest percentage (19.8%) of sentenced female prisoners under state or federal jurisdiction. The imprisonment rate for women was also highest for those ages 35 to 39 (201 per 100,000 women in the U.S. resident population), followed by women ages 30 to 34 (190 per 100,000) (appendix table 14).

State prison capacities were higher in 2008 than in 2000; percent of capacity occupied decreased in 2008

State and federal correctional authorities provide three measures of their facilities' capacity.

Rated capacity is the number of beds or inmates assigned by a rating official to institutions within the jurisdiction.

Operational capacity is the number of inmates that can be accommodated based on a facility's staff, existing programs, and services.

Design capacity is the number of inmates that planners or architects intended for the facility.

Highest capacity is the sum of the maximum number of beds and inmates reported by the states and the federal system across the three capacity measures. Lowest capacity is the minimum of these three capacity measures reported by the states and the federal system. Estimates of prison populations as a percentage of capacity are based on the jurisdiction's custody population. In general a jurisdiction's capacity and custody counts exclude inmates held in private facilities. Some states include prisoners held in private facilities as part of the capacity of their prison systems. Where this occurs, prison population as a percent of capacity includes private prisoners.

The federal system reported a rated capacity of 122,479 beds at yearend 2008 (appendix table 24). The highest capacity reported by the states was 1,272,345, and the lowest capacity reported was 1,139,927 (table 10). These capacities are between 10% and 14% higher than the capacities reported by the states in 2000.

In 2008 the percent of capacity occupied in state prisons decreased. States were operating at 97% of their highest capacity and over 8% of their lowest capacity at yearend. Eighteen states were operating at more than 100% of highest capacity by yearend 2008, and 24 were operating at more than 100% of lowest capacity.

Table 10.

Number of inmates held in custody of state prisons, as a percent of capacity, 1995 and 2000-2008

Year	Highest capacity	Lowest capacity
1995	114%	125%
2000	100	115
2001	101	116
2002	101	117
2003	100	116
2004	99	115
2005	99	114
2006	98	114
2007	96	113
2008	97	109
State capacity, 2008	1,272,345	1,139,927

Note: Capacity excludes prisoners held in local jails and in privately operated facilities, with exceptions. See NPS jurisdiction notes.

Trends in the ICE population

At yearend 2008, U.S. Immigration and Customs Enforcement (ICE) had custody over 34,161 detainees, up 14,646 detainees from yearend 2000 and up 3,730 detainees from yearend 2007 (table 11). The 12.3% growth in the number of detainees in custody of ICE during 2008 was greater than the average annual growth rate (6.6%) of the number of detainees held from 2000 to 2007.

More than half (57.5%) of all detainees were held in facilities in Texas (8,695), California (3,694), Arizona (2,975), Florida (2,195), and Georgia (2,075). The number of detainees held in Texas has increased by 5,080 since 2000, representing 34.7% of the growth in the number of detainees held nationwide (14,646 detainees) during this period.

Nationwide, the overall number of ICE detainees held per facility (state, federal, local, or ICE) has doubled since 2000 (not shown in table). Approximately 53 detainees were held per facility in 2000, compared to about 115 in 2008. The number of state, federal, and local jails responsible for holding this growing population declined from 347 to 256 during this period, and the average number of detainees held per facility increased from approximately 37 to 95. ICE increased its number of facilities from 24 in 2000 to 41 in 2008, while its average number of detainees held per facility fell from about 276 to 243. Texas has independently added a net of three ICE/INS-owned or -contracted facilities since 2000, and increased the number of detainees held in the average Texas facility from approximately 79 in 2000 to 248 in 2008.

Mexican citizens represented over a third (36.2% or 12,360 detainees) of the detainee population in 2008, followed by El Salvadorans (10.3% or 3,521 detainees), Guatemalans (9.4% or 3,227 detainees), and Hondurans (8.1% or 2,780) (figure 6). Among these groups the fastest growth occurred in the Mexican detainee population, increasing from 4,267 ICE detainees in 2000 to 4,623 in 2005. From 2005 to 2007 the Mexican detainee population more than doubled from 4,623 to 10,358 ICE detainees. The number of Mexican detainees increased at a slower pace in 2008, reaching 12,360 at yearend.

While the El Salvadoran detainee population experienced a similar pattern of growth, the population increased at a slower pace during these same periods. The El Salvadoran detainee population rose from 1,125 in 2000 to 1,727 in 2005. From 2005 to 2007 this detainee population increased from 1,727 to 3,005 ICE detainees. During 2008 the El Salvadoran detainee population increased at a slower pace, reaching 3,521 at yearend.

Table 11.

Selected characteristics of ICE detainees and facilities, 2000, 2007, and 2008

Characteristics	Number of detainees			Average annual change, 2000-2007	Percent change, 2007-2008
	2000	2007	2008		
Total	19,515	30,431	34,161	6.6 %	12.3 %
States holding the largest number of detainees					
Texas	3,615	7,842	8,695	11.7 %	10.9 %
California	3,210	3,702	3,694	2.1	-0.2
Arizona	1,685	2,943	2,975	8.3	1.1
Florida	1,491	1,861	2,195	3.2	17.9
Georgia	596	1,452	2,075	13.6	42.9
Facility type					
Intergovernmental service agreement and Bureau of Prisons	12,904	20,711	24,204	7.0 %	16.9 %
ICE owned and contracted	6,611	9,720	9,957	5.7	2.4
Number of facilities	371	326	297		
Intergovernmental service agreement and Bureau of Prisons	347	292	256		
ICE owned and contracted	24	34	41		

Note: Only select characteristics are detailed; categories may not add to totals.

Figure 6.

ICE detainees held, by country of origin, 2000-2008

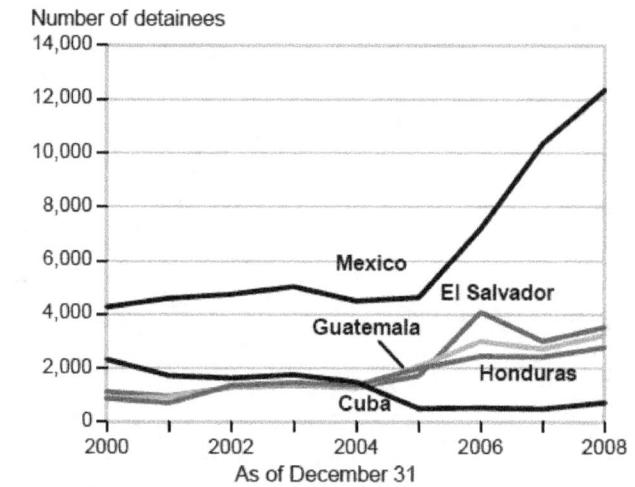

Methodology

National Prisoner Statistics

Begun in 1926 under a mandate from Congress, the National Prisoner Statistics (NPS) program collects statistics on prisoners at midyear and yearend. The Census Bureau serves as the data collection agent for the Bureau of Justice Statistics (BJS). BJS depends entirely upon the voluntary participation by state departments of corrections and the Federal Bureau of Prisons for NPS data.

The NPS distinguishes between prisoners in custody and prisoners under jurisdiction. To have custody of a prisoner, a state or federal prison must hold that prisoner in one of its facilities. To have jurisdiction over a prisoner, a state or federal prison must have legal authority over the prisoner. Some states are unable to provide prisoner counts that distinguish between custody and jurisdiction.

The NPS jurisdiction counts include prisoners serving a sentence within a jurisdiction's facilities. These facilities include prisons, penitentiaries, correctional facilities, halfway houses, boot camps, farms, training/treatment centers, and hospitals. Jurisdiction counts include inmates who are—

• temporarily absent (less than 30 days), out to court, or on work release

• housed in privately-operated facilities, local jails, other state or federal facilities

• serving concurrent sentences for more than one correctional authority.

The NPS custody counts include all inmates held within a respondent's facilities, including inmates housed for other correctional facilities. The custody counts exclude inmates held in local jails and in other jurisdictions. With a few exceptions for several respondents, the NPS custody counts exclude inmates held in privately-operated facilities.

Additionally, NPS data include counts of inmates in combined jail-prison systems in Alaska, Connecticut, Delaware, Hawaii, Rhode Island, and Vermont. The District of Columbia has operated only a jail system since yearend 2001. Prisoners sentenced under the District of Columbia criminal code are housed in federal facilities. Selected previously published prisoner counts and percent population change statistics include DC jail inmates for 2001, the last year of collection. Additional information is provided in notes to the tables, where applicable.

Nevada was not able to provide 2007 data. Estimates were calculated using ratio estimates. All numbers were reviewed and approved by individuals at the Nevada Department of Corrections.

Additional information about the data collection instruments instruments is available online at <http://bjs.ojp.usdoj.gov>.

Military Corrections Statistics

BJS obtains yearend counts of prisoners in the custody of U.S. military authorities from the Department of Defense Corrections Council. The council, composed of representatives from each branch of the military services, adopted a standardized report (DD Form 2720) with a common set of items and definitions in 1994. This report obtains data on persons held in U.S. military confinement facilities inside and outside of the continental United States, by branch of service, gender, race, Hispanic origin, conviction status, sentence length, and offense. It also provides data on the number of facilities and their design and rated capacities.

Other inmate counts

In 1995 BJS began collecting yearend counts of prisoners from the department of corrections in the U.S. Territories (American Samoa, Guam, and the U.S. Virgin Islands) and U.S. Commonwealths (Northern Mariana Islands and Puerto Rico). These counts include all inmates for whom the territory or Commonwealth had legal authority or jurisdiction and all inmates in physical custody (held in prison or local jail facilities). The counts are collected by gender, race, Hispanic origin, and sentence length. Additionally, BJS obtains reports on the design and rated and operational capacities of these correctional facilities.

BJS obtains yearend counts of persons detained by U.S. Immigration and Customs Enforcement (ICE), formerly the U.S. Immigration and Naturalization Service. Located within the Department of Homeland Security, ICE is responsible for holding persons for immigration violations. ICE holds persons in federal, state, and locally operated prisons and jails, as well as privately operated facilities under exclusive contract and ICE-operated facilities.

Data on the number of inmates held in the custody of local jails are from the BJS Annual Survey of Jails (ASJ). The ASJ provides data on inmates in custody at midyear. For more information about the ASJ. (See *Methodology* in *Jail Inmates at Midyear 2008 – Statistical Tables,* BJS Web. 9 Mar. 2009.)

Federal prisoner data used to calculate race and offense distributions are obtained from BJS' Federal Justice Statistics Program (FJSP). The FJSP obtains its data from the Federal Bureau of Prisons. These data include individual-level records of prisoners in federal facilities as of September 30. Specifically, the FJSP provides counts of sentenced federal inmates by gender, race, Hispanic origin, and offense.

Guam did not submit data for 2008. Data for 2008 are estimates based on the percent change from 2006 to 2007 as reported by Guam's Department of Corrections.

Estimates of juvenile inmates for 2007 and 2008 are based on data from 2006 as reported by the Office of Juvenile Justice and Delinquency Prevention (OJJDP), Office of Justice Programs, U.S. Department of Justice.

Estimating changes in admissions and releases

Technically, the change in the prison population from the beginning of the year to the end of the year should equal the difference between the number of admissions and releases during the year. The formula used to calculate this change is $P(t)-P(t-1)=A(t)-R(t)$. Within this formula, t equals the year referenced, $P(t-1)$ equals the start of the year population, $P(t)$ equals the end of the year population, $A(t)$ equals admissions during the year, and $R(t)$ equals releases during the year. However, throughout this report, the references to differences in prison populations refer to the differences between two yearend differences, such as the difference between December 31, 2007, and December 31, 2008. Hence, comparisons of admissions and releases during the year with two yearend population counts may be equal, as there may be changes in the prisoner counts between the last count of the year (December 31) and the first count of the following year (January 1). Also, due to information-system processing issues within states, the two sets of differences do not always equal the difference between the number of admissions and releases for various reasons, such as the final data on admissions and releases may be logged into

systems after the surveys have been submitted to BJS. During the 2008 collections, all but three states submitted data in which the differences between the start of year and yearend populations equaled the difference between admissions and releases.

Estimating age-specific incarceration rates

Estimates are provided for the number of sentenced prisoners under state or federal jurisdiction by gender. Further, prisoners are characterized within genders by age group, race (non-Hispanic white and non-Hispanic black), and Hispanic origin. The detailed race and Hispanic origin categories exclude estimates of persons identifying two or more races.

Estimates were produced separately for prisoners under state or federal jurisdiction and then combined to obtain a total estimated population for 2000 and 2007. State estimates were prepared by combining information about the gender of prisoners from the NPS with information reported during inmate interviews on race and Hispanic origin in the 2004 Survey of Inmates of State Correctional Facilities.

For the estimates of federal prisoners, the distributions of FJSP counts of sentenced federal prisoners by gender, age, race, and Hispanic origin on September 30, 2008, were applied to the NPS counts of sentenced federal prisoners by gender at yearend 2008.

Estimates of the U.S. resident population for January 1, 2009, by age, gender, race, and Hispanic origin, were generated by applying the December 31, 2008, age distributions within gender, race, and Hispanic origin groups to the January 1, 2009, population estimates by gender. The population estimates were provided by the U.S. Census Bureau.

Age-specific rates of imprisonment for each demographic group were calculated by dividing the estimated number of sentenced prisoners within each age group by the estimated number of U.S. residents in each age group. That number was multiplied by 100,000, and then rounded to the nearest whole number. Totals by gender include all prisoners and U.S. residents regardless of racial or Hispanic origin. Detailed race and Hispanic origin imprisonment rates exclude persons identifying two or more races.

Definitions

Average annual change—arithmetic average (mean) annual change across a specific time period.

Custody—physical location in which an inmate is held regardless of which entity has legal authority over an inmates. For example, a local jail may hold, or have custody over, a state-sentenced prisoner who may be held there because of overcrowding. The custody population refers to the number of inmates held in state or federal public prisons or local jails, regardless of sentence length or the state having jurisdiction

Design capacity— the number of inmates that planners or architects intended for a facility.

Highest capacity—the sum of the maximum number of beds reported across three capacity measures: design capacity, operational capacity, and rated capacity.

Imprisonment rate—the number of prisoners under state or federal jurisdiction sentenced to more than 1 year, per 100,000 U.S. resident population.

Incarceration rate—see total incarceration rate.

Inmates—individuals held in the custody of state or federal prisons or in local jails.

Jail—confinement facilities usually administered by a local law enforcement agency, intended for adults but sometimes holding juveniles, before or after adjudication. Facilities include jails and city/county correctional centers, special jail facilities such as medical treatment or release centers, halfway houses, work farms, and temporary holding or lockup facilities that are part of the jail's combined function. Inmates sentenced to jail facilities usually have a sentence of 1 year or less.

Jails in Indian country—jails, confinement facilities, detention centers, and other facilities operated by tribal authorities or the Bureau of Indian Affairs.

Jurisdiction—the entity having legal authority over a prisoner, regardless of where that prisoner is held. The prison population under jurisdiction refers to the number of prisoners under state or federal correctional authority regardless of the facility in which a prisoner is held. For example, state-sentenced prisoners held in local jails are under the jurisdiction of state correctional authorities.

Lowest capacity—the sum of the minimum number of beds across three capacity measures: design capacity, operational capacity, and rated capacity.

Operational capacity—the number of inmates that can be accommodated based on a facility's staff, existing programs, and services.

Prisons—compared to jail facilities, prisons are longer-term facilities run by a state or the federal government typically holding felons and prisoner with sentences of more than 1 year. However, sentence length may vary by state. Connecticut, Rhode Island, Vermont, Delaware, Alaska, and Hawaii operate integrated systems that combine prisons and jails.

Prisoners—individuals confined in correctional facilities under the legal authority (jurisdiction) of state and federal correctional officials.

Rated capacity—the number of beds or inmates assigned by a rating official to institutions within the jurisdiction.

Sentenced prisoner—a prisoner sentenced to more than 1 year.

Total incarceration rate—the number of inmates held in the custody of state or federal prisons or in local jails, per 100,000 U.S. residents.

Total inmates in custody—includes inmates held in any public facility run by a state or the Federal Bureau of Prisons, including halfway houses, camps, farms, training/treatment centers, and hospitals. This number also includes the number of inmates held in local jails as reported by correctional authorities in the Annual Survey of Jails. Data for jails are as of the last weekday of June.

Appendix table contents

NPS jurisdiction notes

Alaska—Prisons and jails form one integrated system. All NPS data include jail and prison populations housed in state and out of state. Jurisdictional counts exclude inmates held in local jails that are operated by communities.

Arizona—Population counts are based on custody data and inmates in contracted beds.

California—Jurisdiction counts include felons and unsentenced inmates who are temporarily absent, i.e. housed in local jails, hospitals, etc. This definition is comparable to the 1998 NPS 1b definition.

Discrepancies between admissions and releases and within-year change in the prison population are due to incomplete data about inmate movements, such as inmates out to court or readmitted on violations.

Colorado—Counts include 222 inmates in the Youthful Offender System, which was established primarily for violent juvenile offenders. Capacity figures exclude seven privately run facilities under contract with the Department of Corrections.

Delaware—Prisons and jails form one integrated system. All NPS data include jail and prison populations.

Federal—Custody counts include inmates housed in secure facilities where the BOP had a direct contract with a private operator or a sub-contract with a private provider at a local government facility. Custody includes inmates held in non-secure privately operated community corrections centers or Halfway Houses and inmates held on home confinement.

Florida—Counts are not comparable to 2006 counts due to new methods of data collection beginning in 2007.

Georgia- Counts are based on custody data.

Hawaii—Prisons and jails form one integrated systems. All NPS data include jail and prison populations

Iowa—Population counts are based on custody data. Population counts for Inmates with a sentence of more than 1 year include an undetermined number of inmates with a sentence of less than 1 year and unsentenced inmates. Iowa does not differentiate between these groups in its data system. Due to a change in reporting in 2006, out of state inmates have been included in jurisdiction counts. Discrepancies between admissions and releases and within-year change in the

prison population are due to data entry corrections made throughout the year.

Kansas—Admission and release data are based on the custody population. Due to a new, computerized reporting system, 2007 admission and release data is not comparable to previous years' counts.

Louisiana—Counts for 2007 are as of December 27, 2007. Custody and jurisdiction counts include evacuees from Hurricane Katrina and other pre-trial offenders from Orleans and Jefferson parish jails.

Maryland—The number of prisoners identifying their race as unknown has increased due to changes in the information system.

Massachusetts—By law, offenders may be sentenced to terms of up to 2.5 years in locally-operated jails and correctional institutions. Such populations are included in counts and rates for local jails and correctional institutions. Counts exclude 4,012 inmates with sentences of more than 1 year held in local jails in 2008 and 6,200 inmates in 2007. Jurisdiction and custody counts include an undetermined number of inmates who were remanded to court, transferred to the custody of another state, federal, or locally-operated system, and subsequently released.

Minnesota—Counts include inmates temporarily housed in local jails or private contract facilities, or on work release and community work crew programs.

Mississippi—Operational and design capacities include private prison capacities.

Missouri—Design capacities are not available for older prisons. Operational capacity is defined as the number of available beds include those temporarily offline. Missouri Department of Corrections does not have updated design capacity for prison extension or improvements.

Montana—Population counts include a small number of inmates with unknown sentence lengths.

Capacity figures include two county operated regional prisons (an estimated 300 beds), one private prison (500 beds), and a state operated boot camp (60 beds). In 2006, the Department of Corrections changed its method of accounting for community corrections offenders placed in residential treatment programs. To track growth patterns, a new standard process was applied to historic

populations, resulting in some changes to previous years' counts.

Nevada—Due to an information system conversion that occurred during 2007, Nevada officials were unable to report data for 2007. All 2007 data were estimated from 2006 reported data. All estimates were reviewed by individuals at the Nevada Department of Corrections.

New Hampshire—Due to a system conversion, detailed information on prisoners sentenced to 1 year or less, unsentenced males, and specific types of admission and releases cannot be captured.

New Jersey—Counts of inmates with a sentence of more than 1 year include an undetermined number of inmates with sentences of 1 year. The Department of Corrections has no jurisdiction over inmates with sentences of less than 1 year or over unsentenced inmates. Rated capacity figures are not maintained.

North Carolina—Capacity figures refer to standard operating capacity, based on single occupancy per cell and 50 square feet per inmate in multiple occupancy units.

Ohio—Counts of inmates with a sentence of more than 1 year include an undetermined number of inmates with sentences of 1 year or less. Due to a system conversion, admission and release data may vary from past years. Returns and conditional releases involving Transitional Control inmates are reported only after movement from confinement to actual release status occurs.

Oklahoma—Population counts for inmates with sentences of less than 1 year consist mainly of offenders ordered by the court to the Delayed Sentencing Program for Young Adults pursuant to 22 O.S. 996 through 996.3. As of November 4, 1998, Oklahoma has one type of capacity, which includes state prisons, private prisons, and contract jails.

Oregon—Counts include an undetermined number of inmates with sentences of 1 year or less. County authorities retain jurisdiction over the majority of these types of inmates.

Pennsylvania—As of May 31, 2004, the Department began using a new capacity reporting system based on design as well as other crucial factors such as facility infrastructure, support services, and programming.

Rhode Island—Prisons and jails form one integrated system. Data reported include jail and prison populations. Improved methods were used to measure admissions and releases during 2007. Admission and release data for 2000 and 2007 are not comparable.

South Carolina—Population counts include 36 inmate who were unsentenced, under safekeeping, or ICC status. As of July 1, 2003, South Carolina Department of Corrections (SCDC) began releasing inmates due for release and housed in SCDC institutions on the 1st day of each month. Since January 1, 2008 was a holiday, inmates eligible for release on January 1 were released on December 31, 2007. Therefore, the inmate count was at its lowest point for the month on December 31, 2007.

South Dakota—Discrepancies between admissions and releases and within-year change in the prison population result because admission and release data is gathered in a separate database than the jurisdiction population data.

Texas—Jurisdiction counts include inmates serving time in a pre-parole transfer (PPT) or intermediary sanctions facility (ISF), substance abuse felony punishment facility (SAFPF), private facilities, halfway houses, temporary releases to counties, and paper-ready inmates in local jails.

Vermont—Prisons and jails form one integrated system. Data reported include jail and prison populations. Improved methods were used to measure admissions and releases during 2007. Admission and release data for 2000 and 2007 are not comparable.

Virginia—Jurisdiction counts are as of December 28, 2007. Rated capacity is the Department of Corrections' count of beds, which takes into account the number of inmates that can be accommodated based on staff, programs, services and design.

Washington—A recently revised law allows increasing numbers of certain inmates with sentences of less than 1 year to be housed in prison.

Wisconsin—Operational capacity excludes contracted local jails, federal and other state and private facilities.

Appendix Table 1.

Prisoners under the jurisdiction of state or federal prisons or in the custody of state or federal prisons or local jails, December 31, 2000-2008

| Year | Prisoners under jurisdiction | | | | | | Imprisonment rate[b] | Incarceration rate[c] |
	Total	Federal	State	Male	Female	Sentenced to more than 1 year[a]		
2000	1,391,261	145,416	1,245,845	1,298,027	93,234	1,331,278	478	684
2001	1,404,032	156,993	1,247,039	1,311,053	92,979	1,345,217	470	685
2002	1,440,144	163,528	1,276,616	1,342,513	97,631	1,380,516	476	701
2003	1,468,601	173,059	1,295,542	1,367,755	100,846	1,408,361	482	712
2004	1,497,100	180,328	1,316,772	1,392,278	104,822	1,433,728	486	723
2005	1,527,929	187,618	1,340,311	1,420,303	107,626	1,462,866	491	737
2006	1,569,945	193,046	1,376,899	1,457,486	112,459	1,504,660	501	751
2007	1,598,245	199,618	1,398,627	1,483,740	114,505	1,532,850	506	756
2008	1,610,446	201,280	1,409,166	1,495,594	114,852	1,540,036	504	754
Average annual change, 2000-2007	2.0%	4.6%	1.7%	1.9%	3.0%	2.0%	0.8%	1.4
Percent change, 2007-2008	0.8	0.8	0.8	0.8	0.3	0.5	-0.3	-0.2

Note: Jurisdiction refers to the legal authority over a prisoner, regardless of where the prisoner is held.
Custody refers to where an inmate is held, regardless of which entity has jurisdiction over the inmate.

[a]Includes prisoners under the legal authority of state or federal correctional officials with sentences of more than 1 year, regardless of where they are held.

[b]Imprisonment rate is the number of prisoners sentenced to more than 1 year under state or federal jurisdiction per 100,000 U.S. residents. Resident population estimates are from the U.S. Census Bureau for January 1 of the following year for the yearend rates.

[c]Incarceration rate is the total number of inmates held in custody of state or federal prisons or local jails per 100,000 U.S. residents.

Appendix Table 2.

Prisoners under the jurisdiction of state or federal correctional authorities, by jurisdiction, December 31, 2000, 2007 and 2008

Region and jurisdiction	Number of prisoners			Average annual change, 2000-2007	Percent change, 2007-2008
	12/31/2000	12/31/2007	12/31/2008		
U.S. total	1,391,261	1,598,245	1,610,446	2.0%	0.8%
Federal	145,416	199,618	201,280	4.6	0.8
State	1,245,845	1,398,627	1,409,166	1.7	0.8
Northeast	174,826	179,030	179,776	0.3%	0.4%
Connecticut[a]	18,355	20,924	20,661	1.9	-1.3
Maine	1,679	2,148	2,195	3.6	2.2
Massachusetts	10,722	11,436	11,408	0.9	-0.2
New Hampshire	2,257	2,943	2,904	3.9	-1.3
New Jersey	29,784	26,827	25,953	-1.5	-3.3
New York	70,199	62,620	60,347	-1.6	-3.6
Pennsylvania	36,847	45,969	50,147	3.2	9.1
Rhode Island[a]	3,286	4,018	4,045	2.9	0.7
Vermont[a]	1,697	2,145	2,116	3.4	-1.4
Midwest	237,378	263,039	263,811	1.5%	0.3%
Illinois	45,281	45,215	45,474	0.0	0.6
Indiana	20,125	27,132	28,322	4.4	4.4
Iowa[b]	7,955	8,732	8,766	1.3	0.4
Kansas	8,344	8,696	8,539	0.6	-1.8
Michigan	47,718	50,233	48,738	0.7	-3.0
Minnesota	6,238	9,468	9,406	6.1	-0.7
Missouri	27,543	29,857	30,186	1.2	1.1
Nebraska	3,895	4,505	4,520	2.1	0.3
North Dakota	1,076	1,416	1,452	4.0	2.5
Ohio	45,833	50,731	51,686	1.5	1.9
South Dakota	2,616	3,311	3,342	3.4	0.9
Wisconsin	20,754	23,743	23,380	1.9	-1.5
South	561,214	639,578	647,312	1.9%	1.2%
Alabama	26,332	29,412	30,508	1.6	3.7
Arkansas	11,915	14,314	14,716	2.7	2.8
Delaware[a]	6,921	7,276	7,075	0.7	-2.8
District of Columbia	7,456	~	~	:	:
Florida	71,319	98,219	102,388	4.7	4.2
Georgia[b]	44,232	54,256	52,719	3.0	-2.8
Kentucky	14,919	22,457	21,706	6.0	-3.3
Louisiana	35,207	37,540	38,381	0.9	2.2
Maryland	23,538	23,433	23,324	-0.1	-0.5
Mississippi	20,241	22,431	22,754	1.5	1.4
North Carolina	31,266	37,970	39,482	2.8	4.0
Oklahoma	23,181	25,849	25,864	1.6	0.1
South Carolina	21,778	24,239	24,326	1.5	0.4
Tennessee	22,166	26,267	27,228	2.5	3.7
Texas	166,719	171,790	172,506	0.4	0.4
Virginia	30,168	38,069	38,276	3.4	0.5
West Virginia	3,856	6,056	6,059	6.7	0.0

Appendix Table 2 (cont.)
Prisoners under the jurisdiction of state or federal correctional authorities, by jurisdiction, December 31, 2000, 2007 and 2008

Region and jurisdiction	Number of prisoners			Average annual change, 2000-2007	Percent change, 2007-2008
	12/31/2000	12/31/2007	12/31/2008		
West	272,427	316,980	318,267	2.2%	0.4%
Alaska[a]	4,173	5,167	5,014	3.1	-3.0
Arizona[b]	26,510	37,746	39,589	5.2	4.9
California	163,001	174,282	173,670	1.0	-0.4
Colorado	16,833	22,841	23,274	4.5	1.9
Hawaii[a]	5,053	5,978	5,955	2.4	-0.4
Idaho	5,535	7,319	7,290	4.1	-0.4
Montana	3,105	3,462	3,607	1.6	4.2
Nevada[c]	10,063	13,400	12,743	:	:
New Mexico	5,342	6,466	6,402	2.8	-1.0
Oregon	10,580	13,948	14,167	4.0	1.6
Utah	5,637	6,515	6,546	2.1	0.5
Washington	14,915	17,772	17,926	2.5	0.9
Wyoming	1,680	2,084	2,084	3.1	0.0

~Not applicable. After 2001, responsibility for sentenced felons from the District of Columbia was transferred to the Federal Bureau of Prisons.

:Not calculated.

[a]Prisons and jails form one integrated system. Data include total jail and prison populations.

[b]Prison population based on custody counts.

[c]Includes estimates for Nevada for December 31, 2007. See *Methodology*.

Male prisoners under the jurisdiction of state or federal correctional authorities, by jurisdiction, December 31, 2000, 2007 and 2008

Region and jurisdiction	Number of male prisoners			Average annual change, 2000-2007	Percent change, 2007-2008
	12/31/2000	12/31/2007	12/31/2008		
U.S. total	1,298,027	1,483,740	1,495,594	1.9%	0.8%
Federal	135,171	186,280	188,007	4.7	0.9
State	1,162,856	1,297,460	1,307,587	1.6	0.8
Northeast	165,744	169,336	169,932	0.3%	0.4%
Connecticut[a]	16,949	19,428	19,159	2.0	-1.4
Maine	1,613	2,009	2,039	3.2	1.5
Massachusetts	10,059	10,646	10,657	0.8	0.1
New Hampshire	2,137	2,741	2,670	3.6	-2.6
New Jersey	28,134	25,417	24,654	-1.4	-3.0
New York	66,919	59,866	57,760	-1.6	-3.5
Pennsylvania	35,268	43,506	47,193	3.0	8.5
Rhode Island[a]	3,048	3,736	3,802	3.0	1.8
Vermont[a]	1,617	1,987	1,998	3.0	0.6
Midwest	222,780	245,110	246,070	1.4%	0.4%
Illinois	42,432	42,391	42,753	0.0	0.9
Indiana	18,673	24,837	25,829	4.2	4.0
Iowa[b]	7,363	8,015	8,017	1.2	0.0
Kansas	7,840	8,071	7,970	0.4	-1.3
Michigan	45,587	48,153	46,781	0.8	-2.8
Minnesota	5,870	8,866	8,778	6.1	-1.0
Missouri	25,550	27,335	27,737	1.0	1.5
Nebraska	3,629	4,106	4,130	1.8	0.6
North Dakota	1,008	1,269	1,292	3.3	1.8
Ohio	43,025	46,909	47,773	1.2	1.8
South Dakota	2,416	2,942	2,987	2.9	1.5
Wisconsin	19,387	22,216	22,023	2.0	-0.9
South	521,562	591,075	598,262	1.8%	1.2%
Alabama	24,506	27,254	28,277	1.5	3.8
Arkansas	11,143	13,248	13,656	2.5	3.1
Delaware[a]	6,324	6,699	6,518	0.8	-2.7
District of Columbia	7,100	~	~	:	:
Florida	67,214	91,365	95,237	4.5	4.2
Georgia[b]	41,474	50,711	49,027	2.9	-3.3
Kentucky	13,858	20,016	19,436	5.4	-2.9
Louisiana	32,988	35,082	35,865	0.9	2.2
Maryland	22,319	22,249	22,264	0.0	0.1
Mississippi	18,572	20,469	20,773	1.4	1.5
North Carolina	29,363	35,344	36,704	2.7	3.8
Oklahoma	20,787	23,242	23,340	1.6	0.4
South Carolina	20,358	22,635	22,693	1.5	0.3
Tennessee	20,797	24,344	25,099	2.3	3.1
Texas	153,097	157,859	158,653	0.4	0.5
Virginia	28,109	35,136	35,309	3.2	0.5
West Virginia	3,553	5,422	5,411	6.2	-0.2

Appendix Table 3. (cont.)
Male prisoners under the jurisdiction of state or federal correctional authorities, by jurisdiction, December 31, 2000, 2007 and 2008

Region and jurisdiction	Number of male prisoners			Average annual change, 2000-2007	Percent change, 2007-2008
	12/31/2000	12/31/2007	12/31/2008		
West	252,770	291,939	293,323	2.1%	0.5%
Alaska[a]	3,889	4,603	4,511	2.4	-2.0
Arizona[b]	24,546	34,286	35,823	4.9	4.5
California	151,840	162,654	162,050	1.0	-0.4
Colorado	15,500	20,506	20,980	4.1	2.3
Hawaii[a]	4,492	5,232	5,227	2.2	-0.1
Idaho	5,042	6,519	6,532	3.7	0.2
Montana	2,799	3,161	3,244	1.8	2.6
Nevada[c]	9,217	12,221	11,761	:	:
New Mexico	4,831	5,890	5,833	2.9	-1.0
Oregon	9,984	12,888	13,058	3.7	1.3
Utah	5,256	5,883	5,906	1.6	0.4
Washington	13,850	16,258	16,522	2.3	1.6
Wyoming	1,524	1,838	1,876	2.7	2.1

~Not applicable. After 2001, responsibility for sentenced felons from the District of Columbia was transferred to the Federal Bureau of Prisons.

[a]Prisons and jails form one integrated system. Data include total jail and prison populations.

[b]Prison population based on custody counts.

[c]Includes estimates for Nevada for December 31, 2007. See *Methodology*.

Appendix Table 4.

Females prisoners under the jurisdiction of state or federal correctional authorities, by jurisdiction, December 31, 2000, 2007 and 2008

Region and jurisdiction	Number of female prisoners			Average annual change, 2000-2007	Percent change, 2007-2008
	12/31/2000	12/31/2007	12/31/2008		
U.S. total	93,234	114,505	114,852	3.0%	0.3%
Federal	10,245	13,338	13,273	3.8	-0.5
State	82,989	101,167	101,579	2.9	0.4
Northeast	9,082	9,694	9,844	0.9%	1.5%
Connecticut[a]	1,406	1,496	1,502	0.9	0.4
Maine	66	139	156	11.2	12.2
Massachusetts	663	790	751	2.5	-4.9
New Hampshire	120	202	234	7.7	15.8
New Jersey	1,650	1,410	1,299	-2.2	-7.9
New York	3,280	2,754	2,587	-2.5	-6.1
Pennsylvania	1,579	2,463	2,954	6.6	19.9
Rhode Island[a]	238	282	243	2.5	-13.8
Vermont[a]	80	158	118	10.2	-25.3
Midwest	14,598	17,929	17,741	3.0%	-1.0%
Illinois	2,849	2,824	2,721	-0.1	-3.6
Indiana	1,452	2,295	2,493	6.8	8.6
Iowa[b]	592	717	749	2.8	4.5
Kansas	504	625	569	3.1	-9.0
Michigan	2,131	2,080	1,957	-0.3	-5.9
Minnesota	368	602	628	7.3	4.3
Missouri	1,993	2,522	2,449	3.4	-2.9
Nebraska	266	399	390	6.0	-2.3
North Dakota	68	147	160	11.6	8.8
Ohio	2,808	3,822	3,913	4.5	2.4
South Dakota	200	369	355	9.1	-3.8
Wisconsin	1,367	1,527	1,357	1.6	-11.1
South	39,652	48,503	49,050	2.9%	1.1%
Alabama	1,826	2,158	2,231	2.4	3.4
Arkansas	772	1,066	1,060	4.7	-0.6
Delaware[a]	597	577	557	-0.5	-3.5
District of Columbia	356	~	~	:	:
Florida	4,105	6,854	7,151	7.6	4.3
Georgia[b]	2,758	3,545	3,692	3.7	4.1
Kentucky	1,061	2,441	2,270	12.6	-7.0
Louisiana	2,219	2,458	2,516	1.5	2.4
Maryland	1,219	1,184	1,060	-0.4	-10.5
Mississippi	1,669	1,962	1,981	2.3	1.0
North Carolina	1,903	2,626	2,778	4.7	5.8
Oklahoma	2,394	2,607	2,524	1.2	-3.2
South Carolina	1,420	1,604	1,633	1.8	1.8
Tennessee	1,369	1,923	2,129	5.0	10.7
Texas	13,622	13,931	13,853	0.3	-0.6
Virginia	2,059	2,933	2,967	5.2	1.2
West Virginia	303	634	648	11.1	2.2

Appendix Table 4. (cont.)
Females prisoners under the jurisdiction of state or federal correctional authorities, by jurisdiction, December 31, 2000, 2007 and 2008

Region and jurisdiction	Number of female prisoners			Average annual change, 2000-2007	Percent change, 2007-2008
	12/31/2000	12/31/2007	12/31/2008		
West	19,657	25,041	24,944	3.5%	-0.4%
Alaska[a]	284	564	503	10.3	-10.8
Arizona[b]	1,964	3,460	3,766	8.4	8.8
California	11,161	11,628	11,620	0.6	-0.1
Colorado	1,333	2,335	2,294	8.3	-1.8
Hawaii[a]	561	746	728	4.2	-2.4
Idaho	493	800	758	7.2	-5.3
Montana	306	301	363	-0.2	20.6
Nevada[c]	846	1,179	982	:	:
New Mexico	511	576	569	1.7	-1.2
Oregon	596	1,060	1,109	8.6	4.6
Utah	381	632	640	7.5	1.3
Washington	1,065	1,514	1,404	5.2	-7.3
Wyoming	156	246	208	6.7	-15.4

~Not applicable.After 2001, responsibility for sentenced felons from the District of Columbia was transferred to the Federal Bureau of Prisons.

:Not calculated.

[a]Prisons and jails form one integrated system. Data include total jail and prison populations.

[b]Prison population based on custody counts.

[c]Includes estimates for Nevada for December 31, 2007. See *Methodology.*

Appendix Table 5.

Sentenced prisoners under the jurisdiction of state or federal correctional authorities, by jurisdiction, December 31, 2000, 2007 and 2008

Region and jurisdiction	Number of sentenced prisoners			Average annual change, 2000-2007	Percent change, 2007-2008
	12/31/2000	12/31/2007	12/31/2008		
U.S. total	1,331,278	1,532,850	1,540,036	2.0%	0.5%
Federal	125,044	179,204	182,333	5.3	1.7
State	1,206,234	1,353,646	1,357,703	1.7	0.3
Northeast	166,632	167,694	168,340	0.1%	0.4%
Connecticut[a]	13,155	14,397	14,271	1.3	-0.9
Maine	1,635	1,950	1,985	2.5	1.8
Massachusetts	9,479	9,872	10,166	0.6	3.0
New Hampshire	2,257	2,930	2,904	3.8	-0.9
New Jersey[b]	29,784	26,827	25,953	-1.5	-3.3
New York	70,199	62,174	59,959	-1.7	-3.6
Pennsylvania	36,844	45,446	48,962	3.0	7.7
Rhode Island[a]	1,966	2,481	2,522	3.4	1.7
Vermont[a]	1,313	1,617	1,618	3.0	0.1
Midwest	236,458	261,391	261,397	1.4%	0.0%
Illinois[b]	45,281	45,215	45,474	0.0	0.6
Indiana	19,811	27,114	28,301	4.6	4.4
Iowa[b,c]	7,955	8,732	8,766	1.3	0.4
Kansas[b]	8,344	8,696	8,539	0.6	-1.8
Michigan	47,718	50,233	48,738	0.7	-3.0
Minnesota	6,238	9,468	9,406	6.1	-0.7
Missouri	27,519	29,844	30,175	1.2	1.1
Nebraska	3,816	4,329	4,424	1.8	2.2
North Dakota	994	1,416	1,452	5.2	2.5
Ohio[b]	45,833	50,731	51,686	1.5	1.9
South Dakota	2,613	3,306	3,333	3.4	0.8
Wisconsin	20,336	22,307	21,103	1.3	-5.4
South	538,997	615,535	617,161	1.9%	0.3%
Alabama	26,034	28,605	29,694	1.4	3.8
Arkansas	11,851	14,310	14,660	2.7	2.4
Delaware[a]	3,937	4,201	4,067	0.9	-3.2
District of Columbia	5,008	~	~	:	:
Florida	71,318	98,219	102,388	4.7	4.2
Georgia[c]	44,141	54,232	52,705	3.0	-2.8
Kentucky	14,919	21,823	21,059	5.6	-3.5
Louisiana	35,207	37,341	37,804	0.8	1.2
Maryland	22,490	22,780	22,749	0.2	-0.1
Mississippi	19,239	21,502	21,698	1.6	0.9
North Carolina	27,043	33,016	34,229	2.9	3.7
Oklahoma	23,181	24,197	24,210	0.6	0.1
South Carolina	21,017	23,314	23,456	1.5	0.6
Tennessee	22,166	26,267	27,228	2.5	3.7
Texas	158,008	161,695	156,979	0.3	-2.9
Virginia	29,643	37,984	38,216	3.6	0.6
West Virginia	3,795	6,049	6,019	6.9	-0.5

Appendix Table 5. (cont.)
Sentenced prisoners under the jurisdiction of state or federal correctional authorities, by jurisdiction, December 31, 2000, 2007 and 2008

Region and jurisdiction	Number of sentenced prisoners			Average annual change, 2000-2007	Percent change, 2007-2008
	12/31/2000	12/31/2007	12/31/2008		
West	264,147	309,026	310,805	2.3%	0.6%
Alaska[a]	2,128	3,072	2,966	5.4	-3.5
Arizona[c]	25,412	35,490	37,188	4.9	4.8
California	160,412	172,856	172,583	1.1	-0.2
Colorado[b]	16,833	22,841	23,274	4.5	1.9
Hawaii[a]	3,553	4,367	4,304	3.0	-1.4
Idaho	5,535	7,319	7,290	4.1	-0.4
Montana	3,105	3,431	3,579	1.4	4.3
Nevada[d]	10,063	13,245	12,743	:	:
New Mexico	4,666	6,225	6,315	4.2	1.4
Oregon[b]	10,553	13,918	14,131	4.0	1.5
Utah	5,541	6,421	6,422	2.1	0.0
Washington	14,666	17,757	17,926	2.8	1.0
Wyoming	1,680	2,084	2,084	3.1	0.0

Note: Totals based on prisoners with a sentence of more than 1 year.

~Not applicable. After 2001, responsibility for sentenced felons from the District of Columbia was transferred to the Federal Bureau of Prisons.

:Not calculated

[a]Prisons and jails form one integrated system. Data include total jail and prison populations.

[b]Includes some prisoners sentenced to 1 year or less.

[c]Prison population based on custody counts.

[d]Includes estimates for Nevada for December 31, 2007. See *Methodology*.

Appendix Table 6.
Number of sentenced male prisoners under the jurisdiction of state and federal correctional authorities, December 31, 2000-2008

Year	Number of sentenced male prisoners			Percent of all sentenced prisoners
	Total	Federal	State	
2000	1,246,234	116,647	1,129,587	93.6%
2001	1,260,033	127,519	1,132,514	93.7
2002	1,291,450	133,732	1,157,718	93.5
2003	1,315,790	142,149	1,173,641	93.4
2004	1,337,730	148,930	1,188,800	93.3
2005	1,364,178	155,678	1,208,500	93.3
2006	1,401,317	162,417	1,238,900	93.1
2007	1,427,064	167,676	1,259,388	93.1
2008	1,434,784	170,755	1,264,029	93.2
Average annual change, 2000-2007	2.0%	5.3%	1.6%	:
Percent change, 2007-2008	0.5	1.8	0.4	:

Note: Totals based on prisoners with a sentence of more than 1 year.
:Not calculated.

Appendix Table 7.

Sentenced male prisoners under the jurisdiction of state or federal correctional authorities, by jurisdiction, December 31, 2000, 2007 and 2008

Region and jurisdiction	Number of sentenced male prisoners			Average annual change, 2000-2007	Percent change, 2007-2008
	12/31/2000	12/31/2007	12/31/2008		
U.S. total	1,246,234	1,427,064	1,434,784	2.0%	0.5%
Federal	116,647	167,676	170,755	5.3	1.8
State	1,129,587	1,259,388	1,264,029	1.6	0.4
Northeast	158,815	159,390	160,004	0.1%	0.4%
Connecticut[a]	12,365	13,581	13,468	1.3	-0.8
Maine	1,573	1,831	1,856	2.2	1.4
Massachusetts	9,250	9,438	9,724	0.3	3.0
New Hampshire	2,137	2,733	2,670	3.6	-2.3
New Jersey[b]	28,134	25,417	24,654	-1.4	-3.0
New York	66,919	59,482	57,412	-1.7	-3.5
Pennsylvania	35,266	43,024	46,261	2.9	7.5
Rhode Island[a]	1,902	2,367	2,418	3.2	2.2
Vermont[a]	1,269	1,517	1,541	2.6	1.6
Midwest	221,902	243,615	243,822	1.3%	0.1%
Illinois[b]	42,432	42,391	42,753	0.0	0.9
Indiana	18,364	24,819	25,808	4.4	4.0
Iowa[b,c]	7,363	8,015	8,017	1.2	0.0
Kansas[b]	7,840	8,071	7,970	0.4	-1.3
Michigan	45,587	48,153	46,781	0.8	-2.8
Minnesota	5,870	8,866	8,778	6.1	-1.0
Missouri	25,531	27,326	27,729	1.0	1.5
Nebraska	3,560	3,963	4,048	1.5	2.1
North Dakota	940	1,269	1,292	4.4	1.8
Ohio[b]	43,025	46,909	47,773	1.2	1.8
South Dakota	2,413	2,937	2,979	2.8	1.4
Wisconsin	18,977	20,896	19,894	1.4	-4.8
South	503,025	571,128	573,111	1.8%	0.3%
Alabama	24,244	26,575	27,567	1.3	3.7
Arkansas	11,084	13,244	13,606	2.6	2.7
Delaware[a]	3,692	3,989	3,862	1.1	-3.2
District of Columbia	4,924	~	~	:	:
Florida	67,213	91,365	95,237	4.5	4.2
Georgia[c]	41,390	50,687	49,014	2.9	-3.3
Kentucky	13,858	19,500	18,906	5.0	-3.0
Louisiana	32,988	34,890	35,324	0.8	1.2
Maryland	21,429	21,640	21,777	0.1	0.6
Mississippi	17,709	19,667	19,855	1.5	1.0
North Carolina	25,654	31,115	32,218	2.8	3.5
Oklahoma	20,787	21,786	21,761	0.7	-0.1
South Carolina	19,716	21,858	21,995	1.5	0.6
Tennessee	20,797	24,344	25,099	2.3	3.1
Texas	146,374	149,995	146,262	0.3	-2.5
Virginia	27,658	35,055	35,249	3.4	0.6
West Virginia	3,508	5,418	5,379	6.4	-0.7

Appendix Table 7. (cont.)
Sentenced male prisoners under the jurisdiction of state or federal correctional authorities, by jurisdiction, December 31, 2000, 2007 and 2008

Region and jurisdiction	Number of sentenced male prisoners			Average annual change, 2000-2007	Percent change, 2007-2008
	12/31/2000	12/31/2007	12/31/2008		
West	245,845	285,255	287,092	2.1 %	0.6 %
Alaska[a]	2,031	2,800	2,704	4.7	-3.4
Arizona[c]	23,623	32,377	33,874	4.6	4.6
California	149,815	161,551	161,220	1.1	-0.2
Colorado[b]	15,500	20,506	20,980	4.1	2.3
Hawaii[a]	3,175	3,863	3,829	2.8	-0.9
Idaho	5,042	6,519	6,532	3.7	0.2
Montana	2,799	3,133	3,218	1.6	2.7
Nevada[d]	9,217	12,068	11,761	:	:
New Mexico	4,322	5,686	5,747	4.0	1.1
Oregon[b]	9,959	12,860	13,026	3.7	1.3
Utah	5,180	5,805	5,803	1.6	0.0
Washington	13,658	16,249	16,522	2.5	1.7
Wyoming	1,524	1,838	1,876	2.7	2.1

Note: Totals based on prisoners with a sentence of more than 1 year.

~Not applicable. After 2001, responsibility for sentenced felons from the District of Columbia was transferred to the Federal Bureau of Prisons.

:Not calculated

[a]Prisons and jails form one integrated system. Data include total jail and prison populations.

[b]Includes some prisoners sentenced to 1 year or less.

[c]Prison population based on custody counts.

[d]Includes estimates for Nevada for December 31, 2007. See *Methodology.*

Number of sentenced female prisoners under the jurisdiction of state or federal correctional authorities, December 31, 2000-2008

Year	Number of sentenced female prisoners			Percent of all sentenced prisoners
	Total	Federal	State	
2000	85,044	8,397	76,647	6.4%
2001	85,184	8,990	76,194	6.3
2002	89,066	9,308	79,758	6.5
2003	92,571	9,770	82,801	6.6
2004	95,998	10,207	85,791	6.7
2005	98,688	10,495	88,193	6.7
2006	103,343	11,116	92,227	6.9
2007	105,786	11,528	94,258	6.9
2008	105,252	11,578	93,674	6.8
Average annual change, 2000-2007	3.2%	4.6%	3.0%	:
Percent change, 2007-2008	-0.5	0.4	-0.6	:

Note: Totals based on prisoners with a sentence of more than 1 year.
:Not calculated.

Appendix Table 9.

Sentenced female prisoners under the jurisdiction of state or federal correctional authorities, by jurisdiction, December 31, 2000, 2007 and 2008

Region and jurisdiction	Number of sentenced female prisoners			Average annual change 2000-2007	Percent change, 2007-2008
	12/31/2000	12/31/2007	12/31/2008		
U.S. total	85,044	105,786	105,252	3.2%	-0.5%
Federal	8,397	11,528	11,578	4.6	0.4
State	76,647	94,258	93,674	3.0	-0.6
Northeast	7,817	8,304	8,336	0.9%	0.4%
Connecticut[a]	790	816	803	0.5	-1.6
Maine	62	119	129	9.8	8.4
Massachusetts	229	434	442	9.6	1.8
New Hampshire	120	197	234	7.3	18.8
New Jersey[b]	1,650	1,410	1,299	-2.2	-7.9
New York	3,280	2,692	2,547	-2.8	-5.4
Pennsylvania	1,578	2,422	2,701	6.3	11.5
Rhode Island[a]	64	114	104	8.6	-8.8
Vermont[a]	44	100	77	12.4	-23.0
Midwest	14,556	17,776	17,575	2.9%	-1.1%
Illinois[b]	2,849	2,824	2,721	-0.1	-3.6
Indiana	1,447	2,295	2,493	6.8	8.6
Iowa[b,c]	592	717	749	2.8	4.5
Kansas[b]	504	625	569	3.1	-9.0
Michigan	2,131	2,080	1,957	-0.3	-5.9
Minnesota	368	602	628	7.3	4.3
Missouri	1,988	2,518	2,446	3.4	-2.9
Nebraska	256	366	376	5.2	2.7
North Dakota	54	147	160	15.4	8.8
Ohio[b]	2,808	3,822	3,913	4.5	2.4
South Dakota	200	369	354	9.1	-4.1
Wisconsin	1,359	1,411	1,209	0.5	-14.3
South	35,972	44,407	44,050	3.1%	-0.8%
Alabama	1,790	2,030	2,127	1.8	4.8
Arkansas	767	1,066	1,054	4.8	-1.1
Delaware[a]	245	212	205	-2.0	-3.3
District of Columbia	84	~	~	:	:
Florida	4,105	6,854	7,151	7.6	4.3
Georgia[c]	2,751	3,545	3,691	3.7	4.1
Kentucky	1,061	2,323	2,153	11.8	-7.3
Louisiana	2,219	2,451	2,480	1.4	1.2
Maryland	1,061	1,140	972	1.0	-14.7
Mississippi	1,530	1,835	1,843	2.6	0.4
North Carolina	1,389	1,901	2,011	4.6	5.8
Oklahoma	2,394	2,411	2,449	0.1	1.6
South Carolina	1,301	1,456	1,461	1.6	0.3
Tennessee	1,369	1,923	2,129	5.0	10.7
Texas	11,634	11,700	10,717	0.1	-8.4
Virginia	1,985	2,929	2,967	5.7	1.3
West Virginia	287	631	640	11.9	1.4

Appendix Table 9. (cont.)
Sentenced female prisoners under the jurisdiction of state or federal correctional authorities, by jurisdiction, December 31, 2000, 2006-2008

Region and jurisdiction	Number of sentenced female prisoners			Average annual change 2000-2007	Percent change, 2007-2008
	12/31/2000	12/31/2007	12/31/2008		
West	18,302	23,771	23,713	3.8 %	-0.2 %
Alaska[a]	97	272	262	15.9	-3.7
Arizona[c]	1,789	3,113	3,314	8.2	6.5
California	10,597	11,305	11,363	0.9	0.5
Colorado[b]	1,333	2,335	2,294	8.3	-1.8
Hawaii[a]	378	504	475	4.2	-5.8
Idaho	493	800	758	7.2	-5.3
Montana	306	298	361	-0.4	21.1
Nevada[d]	846	1,177	982	:	:
New Mexico	344	539	568	6.6	5.4
Oregon[b]	594	1,058	1,105	8.6	4.4
Utah	361	616	619	7.9	0.5
Washington	1,008	1,508	1,404	5.9	-6.9
Wyoming	156	246	208	6.7	-15.4

Note: Totals based on prisoners with a sentence of more than 1 year.

~Not applicable. After 2001 the responsibility for sentenced felons from the District of Columbia was transferred to the Federal Bureau of Prisons.

:Not calculated

[a]Prisons and jails form one integrated system. Data include total jail and prison populations.

[b]Includes some prisoners sentenced to 1 year or less.

[c]Prison population based on custody counts.

[d]Includes estimates for Nevada for December 31, 2007. See *Methodology*.

Appendix Table 10.

Imprisonment rates of sentenced prisoners under jurisdiction
of state and federal correctional authorities, by gender
and jurisdiction, December 31, 2007 and 2008

| Region and jurisdiction | Imprisonment rate | | | | | |
| | 2007 | | | 2008 | | |
	Total	Male	Female	Total	Male	Female
U.S. total[a]	506	955	69	504	952	68
Federal	59	112	8	60	113	7
State[a]	447	844	61	445	840	61
Northeast[b]	306	598	30	306	597	30
Connecticut[c]	410	794	45	407	787	45
Maine	148	284	18	151	289	19
Massachusetts[b]	249	499	13	218	434	13
New Hampshire	222	420	29	220	410	35
New Jersey[d]	308	597	32	298	578	29
New York	322	635	27	307	605	25
Pennsylvania	365	710	38	393	762	42
Rhode Island[c]	235	463	21	240	475	19
Vermont[c]	260	495	32	260	504	24
Midwest	393	743	52	392	741	52
Illinois	350	668	42	351	669	41
Indiana	426	791	71	442	818	77
Iowa[e,d]	291	542	47	291	538	49
Kansas[d]	312	584	44	303	570	40
Michigan	499	971	41	488	951	39
Minnesota	181	341	23	179	336	24
Missouri	506	948	83	509	957	81
Nebraska	243	449	41	247	455	42
North Dakota	221	394	46	225	400	50
Ohio[d]	442	838	65	449	851	66
South Dakota	413	736	92	412	738	87
Wisconsin	397	748	50	374	709	43
South	556	1,050	79	552	1,043	77
Alabama	615	1,180	85	634	1,215	88
Arkansas	502	949	73	511	969	72
Delaware[c]	482	945	47	463	906	45
Florida	535	1,013	73	557	1,054	76
Georgia[e]	563	1,069	72	540	1,021	74
Kentucky	512	934	107	492	902	98
Louisiana	865	1,664	111	853	1,642	109
Maryland	404	793	39	403	796	33
Mississippi	734	1,385	121	735	1,389	121
North Carolina	361	696	41	368	707	42
Oklahoma	665	1,211	131	661	1,203	132
South Carolina	524	1,009	64	519	1,000	63
Tennessee	424	804	61	436	824	66
Texas	669	1,244	97	639	1,191	87
Virginia	490	921	74	489	918	75
West Virginia	333	610	68	331	604	69

Appendix Table 10. (cont.)

Imprisonment rates of sentenced prisoners under jurisdiction of state and federal correctional authorities, by gender and jurisdiction, December 31, 2007 and 2008

Region and jurisdiction	Imprisonment rate					
	2007			2008		
	Total	Male	Female	Total	Male	Female
West[f]	438	807	67	436	803	67
Alaska[c]	447	785	82	430	752	79
Arizona[e]	554	1,009	97	567	1,031	101
California	471	880	62	467	872	62
Colorado[d]	465	829	96	467	834	93
Hawaii[c]	338	594	79	332	585	74
Idaho	483	854	106	474	844	99
Montana	356	649	62	368	660	74
Nevada[f]	:	:	:	486	880	76
New Mexico	313	580	54	316	583	56
Oregon[d]	369	686	56	371	688	58
Utah	239	428	46	232	415	45
Washington	273	500	46	272	501	43
Wyoming	394	686	95	387	687	79

Note: Imprisonment rate is the number of prisoners sentenced to more than 1 year per 100,000 U.S. residents.

[a]The 2008 imprisonment rate includes 4,012 male prisoners sentenced to more than 1 year but held in local jails or houses of corrections in the Commonwealth of Massachusetts. The 2007 imprisonment rate includes 6,200 sentenced males held in local jails or houses of corrections in the Commonwealth of Massachusetts and an estimated number of sentenced prisoners in Nevada. See *Methodology.*

[b]The 2008 imprisonment rate includes 4,012 male prisoners sentenced to more than 1 year but held in local jails or houses of corrections in the Commonwealth of Massachusetts. The 2007 imprisonment rate includes 6,200 sentenced male prisoners held in local jails or houses of corrections in the Commonwealth of Massachusetts.

[c]Prisons and jails form one integrated system. Data include total jail and prison populations.

[d]Includes some prisoners sentenced to one year or less.

[e]Prison population based on custody counts.

[f]The 2007 imprisonment rate includes an estimated number of sentenced prisoners in Nevada. See *Methodology.*

Appendix Table 11.

Number of sentenced prisoners admitted to and released from state or federal jurisdiction, by jurisdiction, December 31, 2000, 2007 and 2008

Region and jurisdiction	Admissions					Releases				
	2000	2007	2008	Average annual change, 2000-2007	Percent change, 2007-2008	2000	2007	2008	Average annual change, 2000-2007	Percent change, 2007-2008
U.S. total	625,219	742,875	739,132	2.5%	-0.5%	604,858	721,161	735,454	2.5%	2.0%
Federal	43,732	53,618	53,662	3.0	0.1	35,259	48,764	52,348	4.7	7.3
State	581,487	689,257	685,470	2.5	-0.5	569,599	672,397	683,106	2.4	1.6
Northeast	67,765	73,283	70,665	1.1%	-3.6%	70,646	71,509	71,413	0.2%	-0.1%
Connecticut	6,185	6,982	6,503	1.7	-6.9	5,918	6,056	6,404	0.3	5.7
Maine	751	1,111	756	5.8	-32.0	677	1,090	720	7.0	-33.9
Massachusetts	2,062	2,670	2,988	3.8	11.9	2,889	2,248	2,667	-3.5	18.6
New Hampshire	1,051	1,290	1,464	3.0	13.5	1,044	1,179	1,507	1.8	27.8
New Jersey	13,653	13,791	12,984	0.1	-5.9	15,362	14,358	13,885	-1.0	-3.3
New York	27,601	26,291	25,302	-0.7	-3.8	28,828	27,009	27,482	-0.9	1.8
Pennsylvania	11,777	17,666	17,493	6.0	-1.0	11,759	16,340	15,618	4.8	-4.4
Rhode Island	3,701	1,120	1,090	:	-2.7	3,223	884	1,086	:	22.9
Vermont	984	2,362	2,273	:	-3.8	946	2,345	2,241	:	-4.4
Midwest	117,776	148,972	146,194	3.4%	-1.9%	114,382	149,826	148,780	3.9%	-0.7%
Illinois	29,344	35,968	36,125	3.0	0.4	28,876	35,737	35,780	3.1	0.1
Indiana	11,876	17,232	18,363	5.5	6.6	11,053	17,099	18,308	6.4	7.1
Iowa	4,656	5,706	5,592	2.9	-2.0	4,379	5,718	5,557	3.9	-2.8
Kansas	5,002	4,849	4,506	-0.4	-7.1	5,231	4,966	4,655	-0.7	-6.3
Michigan	12,169	13,330	12,101	1.3	-9.2	10,874	14,685	13,621	4.4	-7.2
Minnesota	4,406	7,856	7,555	8.6	-3.8	4,244	7,971	7,936	9.4	-0.4
Missouri	14,454	18,300	18,611	3.4	1.7	13,346	19,323	18,864	5.4	-2.4
Nebraska	1,688	2,076	2,059	3.0	-0.8	1,503	1,952	1,963	3.8	0.6
North Dakota	605	1,028	1,085	7.9	5.5	598	977	1,051	7.3	7.6
Ohio	23,780	30,808	29,510	3.8	-4.2	24,793	29,236	28,552	2.4	-2.3
South Dakota	1,400	3,227	3,116	12.7	-3.4	1,327	3,259	3,102	13.7	-4.8
Wisconsin	8,396	8,592	7,571	0.3	-11.9	8,158	8,903	9,391	1.3	5.5
South	217,950	258,223	260,626	2.5%	0.9%	210,777	245,998	257,065	2.2%	4.5%
Alabama	6,296	10,708	11,037	7.9	3.1	7,136	11,079	11,556	6.5	4.3
Arkansas	6,941	6,651	7,017	-0.6	5.5	6,308	6,045	6,610	-0.6	9.3
Delaware	2,709	1,899	1,494	-4.9	-21.3	2,260	1,905	1,617	-2.4	-15.1
Florida	35,683	33,552	40,860	-0.9	21.8	33,994	28,705	37,277	-2.4	29.9
Georgia	17,373	21,134	18,625	2.8	-11.9	14,797	18,774	19,463	3.5	3.7
Kentucky	8,116	15,359	14,273	9.5	-7.1	7,733	13,819	15,413	8.6	11.5
Louisiana	15,735	14,548	15,854	-1.1	9.0	14,536	14,984	14,991	0.4	0.0
Maryland	10,327	10,716	10,396	0.5	-3.0	10,004	10,123	10,383	0.2	2.6
Mississippi	5,796	9,749	7,908	7.7	-18.9	4,940	8,455	7,817	8.0	-7.5
North Carolina	9,848	10,834	11,825	1.4	9.1	9,687	10,074	10,615	0.6	5.4
Oklahoma	7,426	8,795	7,935	2.4	-9.8	6,628	8,486	7,915	3.6	-6.7
South Carolina	8,460	9,912	9,650	2.3	-2.6	8,676	9,461	9,506	1.2	0.5
Tennessee	13,675	14,535	14,196	0.9	-2.3	13,893	15,537	15,414	1.6	-0.8
Texas	58,197	72,525	72,804	3.2	0.4	59,776	73,023	72,168	2.9	-1.2
Virginia	9,791	13,973	13,625	5.2	-2.5	9,148	12,559	13,194	4.6	5.1
West Virginia	1,577	3,333	3,127	11.3	-6.2	1,261	2,969	3,126	13.0	5.3

Appendix Table 11. (cont.)

Number of sentenced prisoners admitted to and released from state or federal jurisdiction,
by jurisdiction, December 31, 2000, 2007 and 2008

Region and jurisdiction	Admissions					Releases				
	2000	2007	2008	Average annual change, 2000-2007	Percent change, 2007-2008	2000	2007	2008	Average annual change, 2000-2007	Percent change, 2007-2008
West	177,996	208,779	207,985	2.3 %	-0.4 %	173,794	205,064	205,848	2.4 %	0.4 %
Alaska	2,427	3,272	3,635	4.4	11.1	2,599	3,286	3,741	3.4	13.8
Arizona	9,560	14,046	14,867	5.7	5.8	9,100	12,560	13,192	4.7	5.0
California	129,640	139,608	140,827	1.1	0.9	129,621	135,920	136,925	0.7	0.7
Colorado	7,036	10,959	11,089	6.5	1.2	5,881	10,604	10,616	8.8	0.1
Hawaii	1,594	1,514	1,731	-0.7	14.3	1,379	1,518	1,795	1.4	18.2
Idaho	3,386	4,055	3,867	2.6	-4.6	2,697	3,850	3,891	5.2	1.1
Montana	1,202	2,055	2,264	8.0	10.2	1,031	2,176	2,117	11.3	-2.7
Nevada*	4,929	6,375	4,610	:	:	4,374	4,904	5,278	:	:
New Mexico	3,161	4,146	4,092	4.0	-1.3	3,383	4,507	4,013	4.2	-11.0
Oregon	4,059	5,331	5,395	4.0	1.2	3,371	5,080	5,055	6.0	-0.5
Utah	3,270	3,466	3,394	0.8	-2.1	2,897	3,393	3,400	2.3	0.2
Washington	7,094	16,478	15,070	12.8	-8.5	6,764	16,488	15,061	13.6	-8.7
Wyoming	638	746	779	2.3	4.4	697	778	764	1.6	-1.8

Note: Totals based on prisoners with a sentence of more than 1 year. Totals exclude escapees, AWOLS, and transfers to and from other jurisdictions.
See *Methodology*.
:Not calculated.
*Includes estimates for Nevada for December 31 2007.

Appendix Table 12.

Number of sentenced prisoners admitted and released from state or federal jurisdiction, by type, December 31, 2008

Region and jurisdiction	Admissions			Releases		
	Total	New court commitments	Parole violators	Total	Conditional releases	Uncondi-tional releases
U.S. total	739,132	478,100	252,707	735,454	506,393	216,276
Federal	53,662	49,270	4,390	52,348	1,225	50,708
State	685,470	428,830	248,317	683,106	505,168	165,568
Northeast	70,665	46,338	22,726	71,413	51,129	18,376
Connecticut	6,503	5,335	1,077	6,404	2,972	3,403
Maine	756	379	377	720	365	355
Massachusetts	2,988	2,678	310	2,667	903	1,735
New Hampshire[a]	1,464	/	/	1,507	/	/
New Jersey	12,984	9,715	3,201	13,885	9,068	4,612
New York	25,302	15,178	10,027	27,482	23,856	3,314
Pennsylvania	17,493	10,564	6,099	15,618	10,396	3,923
Rhode Island	1,090	929	161	1,086	514	567
Vermont	2,273	799	1,474	2,241	2,012	227
Midwest	146,194	97,395	45,649	148,780	117,825	28,858
Illinois	36,125	24,266	11,789	35,780	31,370	4,333
Indiana	18,363	11,165	6,977	18,308	17,778	462
Iowa	5,592	3,073	1,285	5,557	2,880	1,410
Kansas	4,506	3,142	1,341	4,655	3,380	1,246
Michigan	12,101	7,677	3,927	13,621	11,557	1,714
Minnesota	7,555	4,919	2,624	7,936	6,672	1,247
Missouri	18,611	9,952	8,646	18,864	16,618	2,152
Nebraska	2,059	1,789	270	1,963	908	1,042
North Dakota	1,085	733	350	1,051	810	233
Ohio	29,510	24,881	4,606	28,552	14,321	14,107
South Dakota	3,116	1,185	888	3,102	2,744	349
Wisconsin	7,571	4,613	2,946	9,391	8,787	563
South	260,626	193,964	63,708	257,065	148,530	103,046
Alabama	11,037	9,627	1,393	11,556	7,280	4,083
Arkansas	7,017	5,286	1,691	6,610	6,254	311
Delaware	1,494	1,175	291	1,617	1,212	266
Florida	40,860	39,997	116	37,277	12,678	24,303
Georgia	18,625	10,731	7,854	19,463	1,893	17,402
Kentucky	14,273	10,624	3,649	15,413	8,760	6,575
Louisiana	15,854	10,587	4,960	14,991	13,709	1,109
Maryland	10,396	6,520	3,875	10,383	9,429	872
Mississippi	7,908	6,858	1,040	7,817	5,160	1,771
North Carolina	11,825	11,377	419	10,615	3,061	7,388
Oklahoma	7,935	5,530	2,319	7,915	4,353	3,372
South Carolina	9,650	6,483	2,990	9,506	4,926	4,348
Tennessee	14,196	8,425	5,771	15,414	10,129	5,222
Texas	72,804	46,285	25,450	72,168	56,343	13,671
Virginia	13,625	13,001	624	13,194	1,689	11,312
West Virginia	3,127	1,458	1,266	3,126	1,654	1,041

Appendix Table 12. (cont.)
Number of sentenced prisoners admitted and released from state or federal jurisdiction, by type, December 31, 2008

| Region and jurisdiction | Admissions | | | Releases | | |
	Total	New court commitments	Parole violators	Total	Conditional releases	Uncondi-tional releases
West	207,985	91,133	116,234	205,848	187,684	15,288
Alaska[a]	3,635	/	/	3,741	1,709	1,811
Arizona	14,867	12,436	2,377	13,192	10,131	2,181
California	140,827	46,380	94,447	136,925	134,974	1,759
Colorado	11,089	6,355	4,720	10,616	9,021	1,240
Hawaii	1,731	823	908	1,795	658	316
Idaho	3,867	3,584	283	3,891	3,370	500
Montana	2,264	1,920	344	2,117	1,816	284
Nevada[b]	4,610	3,184	1,426	5,278	2,886	2,354
New Mexico	4,092	2,392	1,395	4,013	2,603	1,392
Oregon	5,395	3,703	1,456	5,055	4,796	18
Utah	3,394	1,777	1,617	3,400	2,422	966
Washington	15,070	7,918	7,144	15,061	12,879	2,133
Wyoming	779	661	117	764	419	334

Note: Totals are based on prisoners with a sentence of more than 1 year. Totals exclude transfers, escapes, and AWOLS.

/Not reported.

[a]New reporting systems prevent the disaggregation of admission and/or release type.

[b]Includes estimates for Nevada for December 31 2007.

Appendix Table 13.

Estimated number of sentenced prisoners under state or federal jurisdiction, by gender, race, Hispanic origin, and age, December 31, 2008

Age	Male				Female			
	Total[a]	White[b]	Black[b]	Hispanic	Total[a]	White[b]	Black[b]	Hispanic
Total[c]	1,434,800	477,500	562,800	295,800	105,300	50,700	29,100	17,300
18-19	23,800	6,500	10,400	4,900	1,000	400	300	200
20-24	208,400	59,400	85,000	48,400	11,500	5,400	3,000	2,300
25-29	246,400	66,000	102,800	60,000	16,000	7,300	4,400	3,100
30-34	238,100	70,700	96,800	54,400	18,500	8,900	5,000	3,200
35-39	226,700	75,200	90,500	45,900	20,800	9,900	5,900	3,200
40-44	202,500	75,500	77,400	35,600	17,900	8,700	5,100	2,600
45-49	136,300	53,100	51,300	22,600	10,700	5,200	3,100	1,500
50-54	75,800	31,600	27,000	12,300	5,000	2,500	1,400	700
55-59	39,100	19,000	11,900	6,200	2,100	1,300	500	300
60-64	19,200	10,700	4,700	3,000	1,000	600	200	200
65 or older	15,800	9,300	3,700	2,200	600	400	100	100

Note: Totals based on prisoners with a sentence of more than 1 year. See *Methodology* for estimation method.

[a]Includes American Indians, Alaska Natives, Asians, Native Hawaiians, other Pacific Islanders, and persons identifying two or more races.

[b]Excludes persons of Hispanic or Latino origin.

[c]Includes persons under age 18.

Appendix Table 14.

Estimated rate of sentenced prisoners under state or federal jurisdiction per 100,000 U.S. residents, by gender, race, Hispanic origin, and age, December 31, 2008

Age	Male				Female			
	Total[a]	White[b]	Black[b]	Hispanic	Total[a]	White[b]	Black[b]	Hispanic
Total[c]	952	487	3,161	1,200	68	50	149	75
18-19	528	238	1,532	614	23	16	44	25
20-24	1,916	893	5,553	2,474	112	86	202	131
25-29	2,238	1,017	7,130	2,612	153	115	301	167
30-34	2,366	1,217	8,032	2,411	190	155	380	174
35-39	2,159	1,171	7,392	2,263	201	156	434	183
40-44	1,903	1,090	6,282	2,032	169	127	364	170
45-49	1,202	671	4,056	1,523	93	65	211	106
50-54	713	407	2,385	1,085	45	31	106	61
55-59	429	276	1,325	739	22	18	44	30
60-64	259	184	738	502	12	9	25	23
65 or older	95	69	294	186	3	2	6	4

Note: Totals based on prisoners with a sentence of more than 1 year. Rates are per 100,000 U.S. residents in each reference population group. See *Methodology* for estimation method.

[a]Includes American Indians, Alaska Natives, Asians, Native Hawaiians, other Pacific Islanders, and persons identifying two or more races.

[b]Excludes persons of Hispanic or Latino origin.

[c]Includes persons under age 18.

Appendix Table 15.

Estimated number of sentenced prisoners under state jurisdiction, by offense, gender, race, and Hispanic origin, yearend 2006

Offense	All inmates	Male	Female	White[a]	Black[a]	Hispanic
Total	1,331,100	1,238,900	92,200	474,200	508,700	248,900
Violent	667,900	638,100	29,800	217,100	256,400	145,300
Murder[b]	144,500	135,700	8,800	34,700	61,400	36,800
Manslaughter	16,700	14,900	1,800	6,900	6,100	2,400
Rape	54,800	54,400	400	26,600	16,900	7,400
Other sexual assault	105,500	104,100	1,400	56,800	20,600	23,900
Robbery	179,500	172,400	7,100	37,500	91,500	33,900
Assault	136,600	128,800	7,900	42,800	49,800	34,700
Other violent	30,300	27,800	2,400	11,800	10,100	6,100
Property	277,900	251,200	26,700	135,300	96,000	25,000
Burglary	138,000	132,300	5,700	68,700	53,600	2,800
Larceny	51,600	43,800	7,800	23,300	17,600	7,200
Motor vehicle theft	27,100	25,500	1,600	10,900	7,100	7,900
Fraud	34,400	25,000	9,400	19,200	10,000	2,900
Other property	26,800	24,700	2,100	13,300	7,600	4,200
Drug offenses	265,800	240,500	25,400	72,100	117,600	55,700
Public-order offenses[c]	112,300	106,100	6,200	48,200	35,400	21,000
Other/unspecified[d]	7,200	2,900	4,300	1,400	3,300	1,900

Note: Totals based on prisoners with a sentence of more than 1 year. Detail may not add to total due to rounding. See *Methodology* for estimation method.

[a]Excludes Hispanics and persons identifying two or more races.

[b]Includes negligent manslaughter.

[c]Includes weapons, drunk driving, court offenses, commercialized vice, morals and decency offenses, liquor law violations, and other public-order offenses.

[d]Includes juvenile offenses and other unspecified offense categories.

Appendix Table 16.

Estimated percent of sentenced prisoners under state jurisdiction, by offense, gender, race, and Hispanic origin, yearend 2006

Offense	All inmates	Male	Female	White[a]	Black[a]	Hispanic
Total	100.0%	100.0%	100.0%	100.0%	100.0%	100.0%
Violent	50.2%	51.5%	32.3%	45.8%	50.4%	58.4%
Murder[b]	10.9	11.0	9.5	7.3	12.1	14.8
Manslaughter	1.3	1.2	2.0	1.5	1.2	1.0
Rape	4.1	4.4	0.5	5.6	3.3	3.0
Other sexual assault	7.9	8.4	1.5	12.0	4.1	9.6
Robbery	13.5	13.9	7.7	7.9	18.0	13.6
Assault	10.3	10.4	8.5	9.0	9.8	13.9
Other violent	2.3	2.2	2.6	2.5	2.0	2.5
Property	20.9%	20.3%	28.9%	28.5%	18.9%	10.0%
Burglary	10.4	10.7	6.2	14.5	10.5	1.1
Larceny	3.9	3.5	8.5	4.9	3.5	2.9
Motor vehicle theft	2.0	2.1	1.8	2.3	1.4	3.2
Fraud	2.6	2.0	10.2	4.0	2.0	1.2
Other property	2.0	2.0	2.3	2.8	1.5	1.7
Drug offenses	20.0%	19.4%	27.5%	15.2%	23.1%	22.4%
Public-order offenses[c]	8.4%	8.6%	6.7%	10.2%	7.0%	8.4%
Other/unspecified[d]	0.5%	0.2%	4.6%	0.3%	0.6%	0.8%

Note: Totals based on prisoners with a sentence of more than 1 year. Detail may not add to total due to rounding. See *Methodology* for estimation method.

[a]Excludes Hispanics and persons identifying two or more races.

[b]Includes negligent manslaughter.

[c]Includes weapons, drunk driving, court offenses, commercialized vice, morals and decency offenses, liquor law violations, and other public-order offenses.

[d]Includes juvenile offenses and other unspecified offense categories.

Appendix Table 17.

Number of sentenced prisoners in federal prison, by most serious offense, 2000, 2007 and 2008

Offense	2000	2007	2008	Average annual change, 2000-2007	Percent change, 2007-2008
Total	131,739	179,204	182,333	4.5%	1.7%
Violent offenses	13,740	15,647	15,483	1.9%	-1.0%
Homicide[a]	1,363	2,915	2,949	11.5	1.2
Robbery	9,712	8,966	8,718	-1.1	-2.8
Other violent	2,665	3,767	3,817	5.1	1.3
Property offenses	10,135	10,345	11,080	0.3%	7.1%
Burglary	462	504	475	1.3	-5.7
Fraud	7,506	7,834	7,728	0.6	-1.3
Other property	2,167	2,006	2,876	-1.1	43.4
Drug offenses	74,276	95,446	95,079	3.6%	-0.4%
Public-order offenses	32,325	56,273	59,298	8.2%	5.4%
Immigration	13,676	19,528	19,678	5.2	0.8
Weapons	10,822	25,435	26,942	13	5.9
Other	7,827	11,311	12,678	5.4	12.1
Other/unspecified[b]	1,263	1,492	1,394	2.4%	-6.6%

Note: Based on prisoners with a sentence of more than 1 year. All data are for September 30 from the BJS Federal Justice Statistics Program.

[a]Includes murder, negligent and non-negligent manslaughter.

[b]Includes offenses not classified.

Appendix Table 18.

Number of state or federal prisoners in private facilities, December 31, 2000-2008

Year	Number of prisoners			Percent of all prisoners
	Total	Federal	State	
2000	87,369	15,524	71,845	6.3%
2001	91,828	19,251	72,577	5.8
2002	93,912	20,274	73,638	6.5
2003	95,707	21,865	73,842	6.5
2004	98,628	24,768	73,860	6.6
2005	107,940	27,046	80,894	7.1
2006	113,697	27,726	85,971	7.2
2007	123,942	31,310	92,632	7.8
2008	128,524	33,162	95,362	8.0%
Average annual change, 2000-2007	5.1%	10.5%	3.7%	:
Percent change, 2007-2008	3.7	5.9	2.9	:

:Not calculated.

Appendix Table 19.

Number of state and federal prisoners in private facilities, by jurisdiction, December 31, 2000, 2006-2008

Region and jurisdiction	Number of prisoners			Percent of all prisoners
	12/31/2000	12/31/2007	12/31/2008	12/31/2008
U.S. total	87,369	123,942	128,524	8.0%
Federal[a]	15,524	31,310	33,162	16.5
State	71,845	92,632	95,362	6.8
Northeast	2,509	4,268	4,186	2.3%
Connecticut	0	0	0	0.0
Maine	11	42	0	0.0
Massachusetts	0	0	0	0.0
New Hampshire	0	0	0	0.0
New Jersey[b]	2,498	2,686	2,641	10.2
New York	0	0	0	0.0
Pennsylvania	0	1,022	819	1.6
Rhode Island	0	0	0	0.0
Vermont[b]	0	518	726	34.3
Midwest	7,836	5,048	5,415	2.1%
Illinois	0	/	/	:
Indiana	991	1,683	2,642	9.3
Iowa	0	0	0	0.0
Kansas	0	0	0	0.0
Michigan	449	0	0	0.0
Minnesota	0	1,183	612	6.5
Missouri	0	0	0	0.0
Nebraska	0	0	0	0.0
North Dakota	96	0	0	0.0
Ohio	1,918	2,138	2,133	4.1
South Dakota	45	21	15	0.4
Wisconsin	4,337	23	13	0.1
South	45,560	56,117	57,888	8.9%
Alabama	0	355	101	0.3
Arkansas	1,540	0	0	0
Delaware	0	0	0	0.0
District of Columbia	2,342	~	~	:
Florida	3,912	8,769	9,158	8.9
Georgia	3,746	4,974	5,138	9.7
Kentucky	1,268	2,404	2,209	10.2
Louisiana	3,068	3,004	2,928	7.6
Maryland	127	151	186	0.8
Mississippi	3,230	4,794	5,497	24.2
North Carolina	330	213	217	0.5
Oklahoma	6,931	5,917	5,711	22.1
South Carolina	0	9	12	0.0
Tennessee	3,510	5,121	5,155	18.9
Texas	13,985	18,871	20,041	11.6
Virginia	1,571	1,535	1,535	4.0
West Virginia	0	0	0	0.0

Appendix Table 19. (cont.)
Number of state and federal prisoners in private facilities,
by jurisdiction, December 31, 2000, 2006-2008

| Region and jurisdiction | Number of prisoners | | | Percent of all prisoners |
	12/31/2000	12/31/2007	12/31/2008	12/31/2008
West[a]	15,940	27,199	27,873	8.8%
Alaska	1,383	1,524	1,450	28.9
Arizona	1,430	7,790	8,369	21.1
California	4,547	3,032	3,019	1.7
Colorado	/	4,878	5,274	22.7
Hawaii	1,187	2,129	2,108	35.4
Idaho	1,162	1,969	2,114	29.0
Montana	986	1,324	1,314	36.4
Nevada[c]	508	0	0	0.0
New Mexico	2,155	2,720	2,935	45.8
Oregon	0	0	0	0.0
Utah	208	0	0	0.0
Washington[b]	0	1,203	863	4.8
Wyoming	275	630	427	20.5

:Not calculated.

/Not reported.

~Not applicable. After 2001, responsibility for sentenced felons from the District of Columbia was transferred to the Federal Bureau of Prisons.

[a]Includes federal prisoners held in non-secure, privately operated facilities (8,644 at yearend 2008; numbers from other years can be found in earlier publications).

[b]Includes prisoners held in out-of-state private facilities.

[c]Includes estimates for Nevada for December 31, 2007. See *Methodology*.

Appendix Table 20.
Number of state or federal prisoners in local facilities, December 31, 2000-2008

| Year | Number of prisoners | | | Percent of all prisoners |
	Total	Federal	State	
2000	63,140	2,438	60,702	4.5%
2001	70,681	2,921	67,760	5.0
2002	72,550	3,377	69,173	5.0
2003	73,440	3,278	70,162	5.0
2004	74,445	1,199	73,246	5.0
2005	73,164	1,044	72,120	4.8
2006	77,912	2,010	75,902	5.0
2007	80,621	2,144	78,477	5.0
2008	83,093	2,738	80,355	5.2
Average annual change, 2000-2007	3.6%	-1.8%	3.7%	:
Percent change, 2007-2008	3.1	27.7	2.4	:

:Not calculated

Appendix Table 21.

Number of state and federal prisoners in local jail facilities, by jurisdiction,
December 31, 2000, 2006-2008

Region and jurisdiction	Number of prisoners held in local jails			Percent of all prisoners
	12/31/2000	12/31/2007	12/31/2008	12/31/2008
U.S. total	63,140	80,621	83,093	5.2%
Federal	2,438	2,144	2,738	1.4
State	60,702	78,477	80,355	5.7
Northeast	3,823	1,686	1,454	0.8%
Connecticut[a]	~	~	~	:
Maine	24	9	90	4.1
Massachusetts	457	136	185	1.6
New Hampshire	14	52	46	1.6
New Jersey[b]	3,225	1,468	1,122	4.3
New York	45	21	11	0.0
Pennsylvania	58	0	0	0.0
Rhode Island[a]	~	~	~	:
Vermont[a]	~	~	~	:
Midwest	2,103	3,381	3,567	1.4%
Illinois	0	0	0	0.0
Indiana	1,187	2,002	1,930	6.8
Iowa	0	0	0	0.0
Kansas	0	0	0	0.0
Michigan	286	43	28	0.1
Minnesota	149	518	550	5.8
Missouri	0	0	0	0.0
Nebraska	0	0	0	0.0
North Dakota	38	48	71	4.9
Ohio	0	0	0	0.0
South Dakota	16	55	58	1.7
Wisconsin	427	715	930	4.0
South	49,455	67,071	69,445	10.7%
Alabama	3,401	1,596	1,790	5.9
Arkansas	728	1,007	1,541	10.5
Delaware[a]	~	~	~	:
District of Columbia	1,329	~	~	:
Florida	0	1,147	1,144	1.1
Georgia	3,888	4,919	4,690	8.9
Kentucky	3,850	7,912	7,363	33.9
Louisiana	15,599	17,079	17,524	45.7
Maryland	118	151	141	0.6
Mississippi	3,700	4,952	4,858	21.4
North Carolina	0	0	0	0.0
Oklahoma	970	1,892	2,148	8.3
South Carolina	433	377	361	1.5
Tennessee	5,204	7,019	7,860	28.9
Texas	6,477	12,774	12,805	7.4
Virginia	2,962	5,097	6,057	15.8
West Virginia	796	1,149	1,163	19.2

Appendix Table 21. (cont.)
Number of state and federal prisoners in local jail facilities, by jurisdiction, December 31, 2000, 2006-2008

Region and jurisdiction	Number of prisoners held in local jails			Percent of all prisoners
	12/31/2000	12/31/2007	12/31/2008	12/31/2008
West	5,321	6,339	5,889	1.9 %
Alaska[a]	~	~	~	:
Arizona	237	46	47	0.1
California	2,758	3,023	2,736	1.6
Colorado	2,178	175	63	0.3
Hawaii[a]	~	~	~	:
Idaho	450	575	365	5.0
Montana	548	522	642	17.8
Nevada[c]	175	155	199	1.6
New Mexico	0	116	0	0.0
Oregon	7	23	20	0.1
Utah	1,050	1,286	1,341	20.5
Washington	0	362	430	2.4
Wyoming	17	56	46	2.2

~Not applicable. After 2001, responsibility for sentenced felons from the District of Columbia was transferred to the Federal Bureau of Prisons.

/Not reported.

:Not calculated.

[a]Prisons and jails form one integrated system.

[b]Includes prisoners held in out-of-state private facilities.

[c]Includes estimates for Nevada for December 31, 2007. See *Methodology*.

Appendix Table 22.

Prisoners in custody of correctional authorities in the U.S. territories
and commonwealths, yearend 2007 and 2008

Jurisdiction	Total			Sentenced to more than 1 year			
	2007	2008	Percent change, 2007-2008	2007	2008	Percent change, 2007-2008	Incarceration rate, 2008[a]
Total[b]	14,678	13,576	-7.5%	11,465	10,346	-9.8%	237
American Samoa	236	132	-44.1	122	48	-60.7	74
Guam[b]	535	578	8.1	320	304	-5.0	173
Commonwealth of the Northern Marina Islands	137	124	-9.5	78	78	0.0	141
Commonwealth of Puerto Rico	13,215	12,130	-8.2	10,553	9,642	-8.6	244
U.S. Virgin Islands	555	612	10.3	392	274	-30.1	249

[a]The number of prisoners w th a sentence of more than 1 year per 100,000 persons in the resident population. July 1, 2008 population estimates were provided by the U.S. Census Bureau, International Data Base.

[b]Includes estimates for 2008. Data not available for Guam at time of publication. See *Methodology*.

Appendix Table 23.

Prisoners under military jurisdiction, by branch of service, yearend 2007 and 2008

Branch of service	Total			Sentenced to more than 1 year		
	2007	2008	Percent change, 2007-2008	2007	2008	Percent change, 2007-2008
Total	1,794	1,651	-8.0%	1,089	1,005	-7.7%
To which prisoners belong						
Air Force	280	281	0.4	185	178	-3.8
Army	829	701	-15.4	555	477	-14.1
Marine Corps	396	427	7.8	164	180	9.8
Navy	268	231	-13.8	173	163	-5.8
Coast Guard	21	11	-47.6	12	7	-41.7
Holding prisoners						
Air Force	61	61	0.0	9	9	0.0
Army	912	746	-18.2	721	602	-16.5
Marine Corps	338	351	3.8	97	103	6.2
Navy	483	493	2.1	262	291	11.1

Appendix Table 24.

Reported state and federal prison capacities, December 31, 2008

Region and jurisdiction	Type of capacity measure			Custody population as a percent of—	
	Rated	Operational	Design	Highest capacity[a]	Lowest capacity[a]
Federal	122,479	...	...	135%	135%
Northeast					
Connecticut[b]	...	...	...	...	...
Maine	1,885	1,885	1,885	109%	109%
Massachusetts	...	...	7,959	140	140
New Hampshire	2,145	2,904	2,145	98	133
New Jersey	...	23,022	16,876	96	132
New York	59,830	60,978	57,403	99	105
Pennsylvania	43,298	43,298	43,298	101	101
Rhode Island	4,004	4,004	4,265	88	93
Vermont	1,732	1,470	1,371	80	101
Midwest					
Illinois	34,300	34,300	30,391	133%	150%
Indiana	...	27,084	...	88	88
Iowa	...	...	13,680	64	64
Kansas	9,317	...	...	92	92
Michigan	...	50,462	...	97	97
Minnesota	...	8,361	...	101	101
Missouri	...	31,296	...	96	96
Nebraska	...	3,969	3,175	113	141
North Dakota	1,044	991	1,044	132	139
Ohio	38,320	...	...	127	127
South Dakota	...	3,451	...	97	97
Wisconsin[c]	...	...	17,773	125	125
South					
Alabama[d]	...	25,686	13,403	98%	188%
Arkansas	13,163	13,812	13,163	95	100
Delaware	5,648	5,250	4,161	123	167
Florida[d]	...	102,625	...	88	88
Georgia[e]	...	56,305	...	103	103
Kentucky	13,708	13,708	14,043	93	95
Louisiana[e]	20,857	20,769	...	114	115
Maryland	...	23,638	...	97	97
Mississippi[e]	...	24,019	24,019	75	75
North Carolina[d]	39,529	40,014	34,364	100	116
Oklahoma[e]	25,312	25,312	25,312	94	94
South Carolina	...	24,126	...	98	98
Tennessee	20,408	19,949	...	70	71
Texas[c]	160,371	160,371	164,388	85	87
Virginia	33,250	...	33,250	93	93
West Virginia	4,135	5,017	4,135	98	118

Appendix Table 24. (cont.)
Reported state and federal prison capacities, December 31, 2008

Region and jurisdiction	Type of capacity measure			Custody population as a percent of—	
	Rated	Operational	Design	Highest capacity[a]	Lowest capacity[a]
West					
Alaska	3,058	3,206	...	111 %	116 %
Arizona	35,286	39,292	37,328	79	88
California	...	161,530	84,066	106	204
Colorado	...	14,946	13,055	120	137
Hawaii	...	3,487	2,451	96	137
Idaho[e]	6,534	6,207	6,534	108	113
Montana[c]	...	2,539	...	116	116
Nevada	11,894	10,891	8,689	108	148
New Mexico[e]	...	7,024	6,458	48	52
Oregon	...	14,353	14,353	94	94
Utah	...	6,650	6,886	75	77
Washington	13,777	15,502	15,502	111	125
Wyoming	1,713	1,603	1,598	75	80

...Data not available.

[a]Population counts are based on the number of inmates held in facilities operated by the jurisdiction. Excludes inmates held in local jails, in other states, or in private facilities.

[b]Connecticut no longer reports capac ty because of a law passed in 1995.

[c]Excludes capacity of county facilities and inmates housed in them.

[d]Capacity definition differs from BJS definition, see NPS jurisdiction notes.

[e]Includes capacity of private and contract facilities and inmates housed in them.